AFFORDABLE
PALEO COOKING
WITH YOUR INSTANT POT®

QUICK + CLEAN MEALS ON A BUDGET

JENNIFER ROBINS

BESTSELLING AUTHOR OF *PALEO COOKING WITH YOUR INSTANT POT®*

PAGE STREET
PUBLISHING CO.

PAGE STREET
PUBLISHING CO.

First published in 2018 by

Page Street Publishing Co.

27 Congress Street, Suite 105

Salem, MA 01970

www.pagestreetpublishing.com

Distributed by Macmillan, sales in Canada by The Canadian Manda Group.

22   21   20   19   18   1   2   3   4   5

ISBN-13: 978-1-62414-601-5

ISBN-10: 1-62414-601-5

Library of Congress Control Number: 2018932224

Cover and book design by Page Street Publishing Co.

Photography by Jennifer Robins

Cover photo by Kelly Allison Photography

Printed and bound in China

THIS BOOK IS DEDICATED TO EVERY READER WHO IS PASSIONATELY PURSUING BETTER HEALTH BY COOKING REAL FOOD, EVEN WHEN TIME + BUDGET CONSTRAINTS FEEL DAUNTING. THANK YOU FOR NOT GIVING UP ON ME, ON MY WORK AND ON YOUR OWN COMMITMENTS TO HEALTH + VITALITY. I AM ALONGSIDE YOU ALL THE WAY.

+ CONTENTS +

Introduction — 7

RISE - 9

Pressure-Cooked Scotch Eggs — 11
Two-Faced Avocado Eggs — 12
Migas-Stuffed Acorn Squash — 15
Liver Lovin' Breakfast Porridge — 16
Sweet Potato Bacon Hash + Gravy — 19
Lemon Blueberry Pudding Bowl — 20
Smoky Spaghetti Squash "Frittata" — 23
Golden Milk Breakfast Custard — 24
Potato + Egg Breakfast Cups — 27

OINK + BAA - 53

Egg Roll Meatballs — 55
Deluxe Sausage Pizza Zucchini Boats — 56
Mixed Citrus Pulled Pork — 59
Irish Lamb Stew — 60
Tomatillo Pork — 63
Jamaican Jerk Pork Loin — 64
Sausage + Spinach Soup — 67
Southwest Spicy + Sweet Chili — 68
Southern Sausage + Cabbage — 71
Mustard Chive Bone-In Pork Chops — 72

CLUCK + GOBBLE - 29

Chicken Yum Yum — 31
Chicken Adobo — 32
Crust-less Chicken Pot Pie — 35
Asian Turkey Lettuce Wraps — 36
Chicken Marsala — 39
White Chicken Chili — 40
Chicken Tortilla Soup — 43
Tom Kha Gai — 44
Shredded Caesar Chicken — 47
Thanksgiving Turkey Breast — 48
5 Minute Taco Meat — 51

MOO - 75

Hamburger Soup — 77
Quick + Zesty Enchilada Soup — 78
Mexi Meatloaf — 81
No-Bake Shepherd's Pie — 82
Swedish Meatballs + "Cream" Gravy — 85
Speedy Sloppy Joes — 86
Asian-Inspired Beef + Broccoli — 89
Quick Barbacoa with a Kick — 90
Faux Pho — 93

SPLASH - 95

Cajun Scallops — 97
Crab-Stuffed Mushrooms — 98
Creamy Crawfish Bisque — 101
Hearty Clam Chowder — 102
Cilantro Lime Shrimp Scampi
+ Spaghetti Squash — 105
Seafood Medley Spread — 106
Red Curry Cod — 109
Roux-less Gumbo — 110
Chili Lime Salmon — 113

SPROUT - 115

Turmeric Tomato Detox Soup — 117
Minute Mashed Parsnips — 118
Crispy Ghee-licious Smashed Potatoes — 121
Old Country Beet Borsht — 122
Indian-Inspired "Butter" Cauliflower — 125
Popeye Soup — 126
Loaded Egg Drop Soup — 129
Quickest French Onion Soup — 130
Buttered Carrot Bisque — 133
Dairy-Free Broccoli "Cheese" Soup — 134
Creamy Asparagus Soup — 137
Quick-Pickled Onions — 138
Hot Minute Spinach + Artichoke Dip — 141
Creamy Tahini Zoodles — 142

SLURP + DRIZZLE - 145

Beef Broth — 147
Chicken Broth — 148
Vegetable Broth — 151
Umami Broth — 152
Queso Dip — 155
Date-Sweetened BBQ Sauce — 156
Pesto "Cream" Sauce — 159
Hot Minute Pepper Jelly — 160
Garlic-Infused Ghee — 163
5 Minute Easy Adobo Sauce — 164
Cream-less Cream Gravy — 167
Sausage Gravy — 168

Acknowledgments — 170
About the Author — 171
Index — 172

✛ INTRODUCTION ✛

Here we are again! Just as I thought my cookbook-writing days were over, I'm back. As it turns out, people can't get enough of their Instant Pots® and other pressure cookers, proving once again that even though we are short on time we are long on desire to prepare healthy meals for ourselves and our families. Our days are full the stakes are high and the devotion is still there to make sure we are putting good stuff into our bodies.

So here I am! After the popularity of *Paleo Cooking with Your Instant Pot*®, it appears you Instant Potters are here to stay, and you want more recipes. I've been talking to you and listening to your feedback, and from what I've gathered you need meals that are quick, healthy, cost effective, easy to freeze and reheat and that contain easily accessible ingredients you can find at almost any mainstream grocery store. You also seem to be looking for recipes that accommodate special diets such as 21-Day Sugar Detox (21DSD), Paleo, Keto, Low Carb, Vegetarian and Autoimmune Protocol (AIP).

After lots of brainstorming, hand-wringing and meditating, I've come up with a ton of brand-new recipes that fit the aforementioned requirements. I am beyond enthused to share them with you.

Here are a few notes I'd like to mention: First, you'll find labels at the top of each recipe that indicate which specialty diet it falls under. Some recipes even hit all the categories! Second, I've written the recipes so that if you are cooking with a different brand of electric pressure cooker than the Instant Pot, you should still find the instructions easy to follow. They are all cooked with manual instructions at high pressure using the quick-release method, so you won't need to do much finagling with your settings. Third, the majority of these recipes can be frozen right after you make them, so you can cook ahead and store for later. Fourth, these recipes contain no specialty ingredients, no sweeteners other than fruit, no Paleo flours and no nuts of any kind. You should be able to go to almost any neighborhood grocery store and find the ingredients I'm using here. Fifth, I've written this book with budget in mind. While I do prefer to use pastured, grass-fed meats and organic vegetables, you can choose less expensive ingredients in order to accommodate your personal needs.

I'm hoping this book helps take the guesswork out of meal time and the stress out of preparing healthy food, and that it puts the ease back into eating whole foods. Here's to your health! No pressure, y'all!

jen

RISE

THEY SAY BREAKFAST IS THE MOST IMPORTANT MEAL OF THE DAY, and yet people often feel completely uninspired when it comes to their morning fare. For those who get tired of eating the same meal daily, this chapter is for you. Choose from unique Instant Pot concepts like Pressure-Cooked Scotch Eggs (page 11) or my egg-free Golden Milk Breakfast Custard (page 24). Make these recipes in advance so you can grab and go during busy weekday mornings. You'll find recipes suitable to a variety of nutritional lifestyles, and no shortage of different ideas!

PRESSURE-COOKED SCOTCH EGGS

+PALEO +21DSD +LOW CARB +KETO

+ MAKES 5 SERVINGS +
PREP TIME: 10 MINUTES
COOK TIME: 9 MINUTES

Scotch eggs are a great way to pack in lots of savory protein and good fats. There are different ways to prepare them—breaded, fried, soft or hard boiled—but the end result is always a satisfyingly delicious way to start (or end) the day!

1 cup (240 ml) water

5 eggs

2 cups (480 ml) ice water

1 lb (450 g) high quality ground breakfast sausage (pastured when possible)

1. Pour the water into the stainless steel bowl of your Instant Pot, lower the trivet/steamer tray into the bowl and place your eggs on it. Secure the lid and close off the pressure valve. Press the Pressure Cook/Manual button and then the +/- buttons until 5 minutes is displayed.

2. Allow the cooking cycle to complete, then quick release the pressure valve and remove the lid when safe to do so. Use a slotted spoon or skimmer to remove the eggs and immediately place them in the ice water for 2 minutes. While the eggs cool, divide your sausage up into 5 equal parts.

3. Once the eggs are cool, carefully peel them. Take one portion of the sausage and press or roll it flat until it is about ¼ inch (6 mm) thick. Use this sausage to wrap around one egg entirely, making sure there are no holes or cracks. Place it on the trivet/steamer tray in the Instant Pot with the seam side down so it does not open while cooking. Repeat with the remaining eggs and sausage.

4. Secure the lid, close the pressure valve and press the Keep Warm/Cancel button. Press the Pressure Cook/Manual button and then the +/- buttons until 4 minutes is displayed.

5. Allow the cooking cycle to complete and then quick release the pressure valve and remove the lid when safe to do so. Serve warm, or refrigerate and reheat them throughout the week.

TWO-FACED AVOCADO EGGS

+PALEO +21DSD +LOW CARB +VEGETARIAN +KETO

+ MAKES: 4 SERVINGS +
PREP TIME: 5 MINUTES
COOK TIME: 4 MINUTES

Don't worry, these eggs won't talk about you behind your back—but they do combine the best of both worlds by being a little runny and a little hard-boiled. Add in an unlikely avocado friend, and you've got a breakfast of healthy fats and protein in minutes!

2 avocados

4 eggs

¼ tsp paprika

Sea salt and pepper

1 cup (240 ml) water

Fresh parsley or cilantro (optional)

1. Slice open the avocados lengthwise, then remove and discard the pits.

2. Crack open an egg and gently discard or reserve the white without breaking open the yolk. Ease the yolk into the opening of one halved avocado and set it aside, then repeat with the remaining eggs and avocado halves. Sprinkle with the paprika and your desired amount of sea salt and pepper.

3. Pour the water into the stainless steel bowl of your Instant Pot and lower in the trivet. Place the egg-filled avocados onto the trivet carefully. Press the Pressure Cook/Manual button and the +/- buttons until 4 minutes is displayed.

4. Allow the cooking cycle to complete, then quick release the pressure valve and remove the lid once safe to do so. Carefully remove the egg-filled avocados and eat them immediately or refrigerate them for later. Garnish with fresh parsley or cilantro if desired.

MIGAS-STUFFED ACORN SQUASH

+PALEO +21DSD +LOW CARB +VEGETARIAN

+ MAKES: 2 SERVINGS +
PREP TIME: 5 MINUTES
COOK TIME: 10 MINUTES

1 cup (240 ml) water

1 acorn squash, sliced in half vertically and seeded

2 eggs, whisked

¼ cup (60 g) salsa

½ tsp onion powder

½ tsp garlic powder

½ tsp chipotle powder or cumin

1 tbsp (14 g) ghee

½ tsp sea salt

Fresh chopped cilantro (optional)

Sliced avocado (optional)

Diced peppers (optional)

When my neighbor showed up with a bowl full of squash, peppers and avocados she wouldn't be able to use, I knew I had to get busy quickly to avoid any waste. I had the idea to use one of my favorite breakfasts, migas, to fill up this beautiful acorn squash. Though it is certainly different than the traditional preparation, it was delicious nonetheless!

1. Pour the water into the stainless steel bowl of your Instant Pot, then lower in the trivet and position your hollowed acorn squash halves onto it. You may want to use a piece of crumpled foil to help stabilize the halves so they do not tip over. You'll want them stable before you fill them otherwise the eggs will pour out during the cooking process.

2. Combine the eggs, salsa, onion powder, garlic powder, chipotle powder, ghee and sea salt in a bowl and mix well.

3. Spoon or pour the egg mixture into the acorn squash halves. Secure the lid and close the pressure valve. Press the Pressure Cook/Manual button and use the +/- buttons to adjust the time until 10 minutes is displayed.

4. Allow the cooking cycle to complete and then quick release the pressure valve. Remove the lid once safe to do so and carefully remove the acorn squash. Top with cilantro, avocado or diced peppers, if desired.

LIVER LOVIN' BREAKFAST PORRIDGE

+PALEO +AIP +VEGETARIAN

+ MAKES: 4 SERVINGS +
PREP TIME: 5 MINUTES
COOK TIME: 5 MINUTES

You won't find any sweeteners or food dyes in this pretty breakfast idea. But you will find lots of whole food nutrition and loads of micronutrients, which are great for liver support. This one is super kid-friendly too and is free of eggs for those choosing to avoid them.

½ small beet

2 bananas (less ripe)

½ cup (120 ml) full-fat coconut milk

6 oz (170 g) fresh raspberries

¼ cup (60 ml) pomegranate juice

½ tsp vanilla extract (no alcohol)

1 light green apple, cored

1. Place all of the ingredients into the stainless steel bowl of your Instant Pot. Secure the lid, close the pressure valve and press the Pressure Cook/Manual button, then press the +/- button until 5 minutes is displayed.

2. Allow the cooking cycle to complete, then quick release the pressure valve and remove the lid once safe to do so. Puree the contents with an immersion blender or transfer to a standing blender.

3. Serve the porridge warm or chilled, and top it with additional fresh fruit if you desire.

SWEET POTATO BACON HASH + GRAVY

+PALEO +21DSD +AIP

+ MAKES: 4 SERVINGS +
PREP TIME: 5 MINUTES
COOK TIME: 15 MINUTES

This quick hash is a great way to start the morning, and it's also egg free for those on restricted diets. It's full of flavor and clean ingredients, plus has healthy carbs to fuel your day and it's so tasty you may find yourself making extra so you can eat it for lunch too!

1 tbsp (14 g) ghee, avocado oil or olive oil (avoid ghee for AIP)

1 (8-oz [225-g]) package bacon, chopped

1 large onion, diced

18 oz (500 g or 3 cups) sweet potato, diced or cubed

½ tsp onion powder

½ tsp garlic powder

¾ cup (180 ml) Beef Broth (page 147)

Sea salt to taste

1. Drizzle the ghee or oil into the stainless steel bowl of your Instant Pot and press the Sauté button. Add the bacon and onion and cook, shifting often so they do not stick, for about 5 to 8 minutes.

2. Add in the remaining ingredients. Press the Keep Warm/Cancel button, secure the lid and close the pressure valve, then press the Pressure Cook/Manual button. Use the +/- buttons until 5 minutes is displayed.

3. Allow the cooking cycle to complete, then quick release the pressure valve and remove the lid once safe to do so. Using a slotted spoon or skimmer, remove the sweet potato bacon hash and leave the liquid.

4. Press the Keep Warm/Cancel button and then the Sauté button. Allow the liquid to simmer until it reduces to a gravy consistency, around 5 to 10 minutes. Serve the hash topped with the gravy.

LEMON BLUEBERRY PUDDING BOWL

+PALEO +AIP

+ MAKES: 4 SERVINGS +
PREP TIME: 5 MINUTES
COOK TIME: 5 MINUTES

When the craving comes on for something light, slightly sweet and packed with nutrition, this is your answer. It's sweetened only with fruit and has healthy fats to balance those carbs. Plus, it's easy on the eyes!

⅔ cup (160 ml) 100% white grape juice (or regular grape juice)

1 (14-oz [385-ml]) can full-fat coconut milk

2 lemons, juiced

6 oz (170 g) blueberries

Pinch of sea salt

2 tbsp (28 g) gelatin (not collagen)

1. Start by combining all of the ingredients except for the gelatin in the stainless steel bowl of your Instant Pot. Secure the lid, close the pressure valve and press the Pressure/Cook Manual button. Press the +/- buttons until 5 minutes is displayed.

2. Allow the cooking time to complete, then quick release the pressure valve and remove the lid once safe to do so. Puree the mixture using an immersion blender or transfer to a vertical blender.

3. Sprinkle in the gelatin and blend again, making sure to dissolve any lumps.

4. Pour the mixture into individual serving cups and refrigerate until it sets, around 1 hour or more. This can be made ahead and eaten throughout the week.

SMOKY SPAGHETTI SQUASH "FRITTATA"

+PALEO +21DSD +LOW CARB +VEGETARIAN

+ MAKES: 4 SERVINGS +
PREP TIME: 10 MINUTES
COOK TIME: 29 MINUTES

Okay, so this is probably not the frittata recipe you learned, but it's a great hands-off option that will allow you to catch up on your favorite show instead of babysitting your breakfast. The smoked paprika adds a little something different for a full-bodied flavor and a kick to start the day.

1 cup (240 ml) water

1 small/medium spaghetti squash, sliced across the shortest part (you'll need to yield about 2 cups [240 g] of actual cooked spaghetti "strands")

4 eggs

½ onion, minced

1 tbsp (14 g) melted ghee, avocado oil or olive oil

½ tsp sea salt

½ tsp dried parsley

½ tsp ground black pepper

½ tsp onion powder

½ tsp garlic powder

½ tsp smoked paprika

1. Pour the water into the stainless steel bowl of your Instant Pot, then lower your steaming tray/trivet. Place the spaghetti squash sliced-side down onto the trivet—the halves can be stacked if necessary. Secure the lid and close the pressure valve. Press the Pressure Cook/Manual button and then the +/- buttons until 9 minutes is displayed.

2. Allow the cooking cycle to complete, then quick release the pressure valve and remove the lid once safe to do so. Carefully remove the cooked spaghetti squash using a utensil since it is very hot. Press the Keep Warm/Cancel button.

3. Allow the squash to cool slightly and then scoop out the strands from the spaghetti squash using a fork. Discard the seeds and place the strands in a mixing bowl. Add the remaining ingredients to the bowl and stir to combine.

4. Spoon the mixture into a 3-cup (700-ml), pressure cooker–safe casserole dish (high-heat tolerant tempered glass or silicone work well) and lower the dish onto the trivet, covering it tightly with foil.

5. Press the Manual/Pressure Cook button and then press the +/- button until 20 minutes is displayed. Allow the cooking cycle to complete, then quick release the pressure valve and remove the lid once safe to do so. Slice and serve or refrigerate for later.

GOLDEN MILK BREAKFAST CUSTARD

+PALEO +AIP

+ MAKES: 4 SERVINGS +
PREP TIME: 5 MINUTES
COOK TIME: 5 MINUTES

Turmeric is a powerful healing tool in Ayurvedic medicine, and fortunately it is delicious too! This breakfast custard is great to make ahead, refrigerate and eat throughout the week in individual servings.

1 (14-oz [385-ml]) can full-fat coconut milk

3 dates, pitted

1 tsp ground turmeric

1 tsp vanilla extract (alcohol free for AIP)

2 tbsp (28 g) ghee (or avocado oil for AIP)

Pinch of sea salt

1 tbsp (14 g) gelatin (not collagen)

Fresh fruit and coconut cream, for serving (optional)

1. Combine all of the ingredients except the gelatin in the stainless steel bowl of your Instant Pot and give them a quick stir. Secure the lid, close the pressure valve and press the Pressure Cook/Manual button, then press the +/- buttons until the display reads 5 minutes.

2. Allow the cooking cycle to complete, then quick release the pressure valve and remove the lid once safe to do so. Use an immersion blender or standing blender to puree the ingredients, adding in the gelatin as you do.

3. Transfer the custard to one large bowl or several individual bowls, cover and refrigerate them for around 1 hour or until the custard is set. Top it with fresh fruit or coconut cream if you desire.

POTATO + EGG BREAKFAST CUPS

+PALEO +21DSD +VEGETARIAN

> **+ MAKES: 3 LARGE OR 5 +**
> **SMALLER SERVINGS**
> **PREP TIME: 5 MINUTES**
> **COOK TIME: 14 MINUTES**

These are the absolute perfect grab and go breakfast items for during the week. They are easy to prepare, and if you make them in individual silicone muffin cups, they can be transferred from Instant Pot to fridge for a weeklong breakfast stash!

1 cup (180 g) shredded potato

5 eggs, whisked

2 tsp (28 g) ghee

1 tsp sea salt

½ tsp pepper

½ tsp onion powder

½ tsp garlic powder

1 cup (240 ml) water

1. Combine all of the ingredients except the water in a bowl and stir well. Divide the mixture evenly between 3 large individual silicone muffin cups or 5 standard-size muffin cups.

2. Pour the water into the stainless steel bowl of your Instant Pot. Lower in the trivet and place your filled muffin cups on top. If you have limited space, you can also carefully stack the muffin cups. Secure the lid, close the pressure valve and press the Pressure Cook/Manual button. Use the +/- buttons to adjust the time until 14 minutes is displayed.

3. Allow the cooking cycle to complete, then quick release the pressure valve and remove the lid once safe to do so. Carefully remove the muffin cups and serve them warm, or chill and eat them throughout the week.

CLUCK + GOBBLE

CAN I BE HONEST FOR A MINUTE HERE? Chicken and poultry dishes can get really, ahem, boring. Remember the steamed chicken breast and broccoli craze? Yawn. You could not have paid me to choke down another piece of dry, flavorless meat. And by the way, show me a little fat would you! Dried-out protein is not my jam, so I imagine there are plenty of you who also get in some good eye-cardio from rolling your eyeballs at all the poultry "recipes" out there.

This chapter is dedicated to all the sad, overcooked chicken recipes that made for lots of frowny faces at the dinner table. I promise you that you'll find none of those in here. I am committed to flavor, personality and crowd pleasers, not just because I am a chicken snob, but also because I hate looking at the "meh" faces my kids make if I under deliver. That's an expression no mom wants to deal with, am I right?

CHICKEN YUM YUM

+PALEO

⁺ MAKES: 4 SERVINGS ⁺
PREP TIME: 2 MINUTES
COOK TIME: 12 MINUTES

When I created this recipe for the blog, it quickly became one of my most popular recipes to date. In this version of that favorite original, I've taken out the high-quality ketchup and the maple syrup or honey to make it even more compliant with your favorite eating plans.

6 dates, pitted

½ cup (120 ml) tomato sauce

¼ cup (60 ml) coconut aminos

¼ cup (54 g) ghee

1 tbsp (10 g) minced garlic

1 tsp sea salt

¾ cup (180 ml) Chicken Broth (page 148)

2 lbs (900 g) boneless chicken thighs

1. Combine all of the ingredients except the chicken thighs and puree them in a blender until smooth.

2. Place the chicken into the stainless steel bowl of your Instant Pot and pour in the sauce. Give it a quick stir and then secure the lid, close the pressure valve and press the Pressure Cook/Manual button. Use the +/- buttons to adjust the time until 12 minutes is displayed.

3. Allow the cooking cycle to complete, then quick release the pressure valve and remove the lid once safe to do so. Shred the chicken with two forks and serve it with the sauce on top—try it on some mashed or roasted cauliflower!

CHICKEN ADOBO

+PALEO +21DSD +LOW CARB +AIP +KETO

+ MAKES: 4 SERVINGS +
PREP TIME: 5 MINUTES
COOK TIME: 12 MINUTES

This recipe is such a delightful treat, and it's far more flavorful than you'd ever expect from the short list of ingredients! This is also a great one for entertaining; just double, triple or quadruple the ingredients for a crowd pleaser all around.

2 lbs (900 g) boneless chicken thighs

½ cup (120 ml) coconut aminos

½ cup (120 ml) coconut milk

3 tbsp (45 ml) apple cider vinegar

4 tbsp (40 g) chopped garlic

1 tsp sea salt

2 tbsp (30 ml) olive oil, avocado oil or ghee

2 bay leaves

1 tsp ground black pepper (omit for AIP)

1. Place all of the ingredients in a zip-top bag and shake it to combine them, then allow the chicken to marinate in the refrigerator for a few hours if time allows.

2. Empty all of the ingredients into your pressure cooker. Secure the lid and close the pressure valve, then press the Pressure Cook/Manual button and adjust the time with the +/- buttons until 12 minutes is displayed.

3. Allow the cooking cycle to complete, then quick release the pressure valve and remove the lid once safe to do so. Remove the chicken thighs and shred them with two forks onto a plate.

4. Press the Keep Warm/Cancel button and then the Sauté button. Allow the sauce to reduce until it thickens slightly, around 8 minutes. Drizzle the sauce over the top of the chicken before serving.

CRUST-LESS CHICKEN POT PIE

+PALEO +21DSD +AIP +LOW CARB

+ MAKES: 6 SERVINGS +
PREP TIME: 5 MINUTES
COOK TIME: 15 MINUTES

Skipping the crust on chicken pot pie might seem like the worst idea possible, but what if I told you that the savory, hearty filling can be made to accommodate almost any dietary need AND that you'd hardly miss the crust? You'd go for it, you know you would.

4 cups (960 ml) Chicken Broth (page 148)

2 heads cauliflower, florets only

1 lb (450 g) boneless chicken breast, chopped into bite-sized pieces

2 small white-fleshed sweet potatoes, diced

2 celery ribs, chopped

2 cups (300 g) chopped carrots

1 tbsp (9 g) minced garlic

1 large onion, diced

1 tsp onion powder

2 tsp (12 g) sea salt

2 bay leaves

1 large sprig fresh thyme (optional)

Chives (optional)

1. Pour the chicken broth into the stainless steel bowl of your Instant Pot, then place in the cauliflower, close the lid and close the pressure valve. Press the Pressure Cook/Manual button then press the +/- buttons until 5 minutes is displayed.

2. Allow the cooking cycle to complete, quick release the pressure valve and remove the lid once safe to do so. Press the Keep Warm/Cancel button.

3. Puree the cauliflower and broth with an immersion blender or transfer to a stand mixer to do so.

4. Add in the remaining ingredients, except the thyme and chives, and secure the lid and pressure valve. Press the Pressure Cook/Manual button and then use the +/- buttons to adjust the time to 10 minutes.

5. Allow the cooking cycle to complete, then quick release the pressure valve and remove the lid once safe to do so. Remove the bay leaves. Serve topped with fresh thyme, chives or your preferred fresh herbs.

ASIAN TURKEY LETTUCE WRAPS

+PALEO +21DSD +LOW CARB +AIP +KETO

+ MAKES: 5 SERVINGS +
PREP TIME: 5 MINUTES
COOK TIME: 15 MINUTES

I love this recipe not just for its ease or its savory combination of flavors, but because you can likely find all the ingredients in your fridge and pantry when you are feeling uninspired and overwhelmed. This no-fuss meal is on your table in minutes and is one just about everyone loves!

3 tbsp (45 ml) olive oil or avocado oil

1 tsp sesame oil (omit for AIP)

1 large onion, diced

10 oz (280 g) button mushrooms, diced

1 lb (450 g) ground turkey

3 tsp (9 g) minced garlic

1 tsp hot sauce (omit for AIP)

½ cup (120 ml) coconut aminos

1 tsp onion powder

1 tsp sea salt

1 tsp mustard powder (omit for AIP)

12 oz (340 g) whole hearts of romaine

Minced chives (optional)

Shredded carrots (optional)

1. Begin by drizzling the cooking oils into the stainless steel bowl of your Instant Pot, then press the Sauté button and add in the onion and mushrooms. Allow them to cook for about 5 minutes, until they start to release water.

2. Add in the ground turkey, garlic, hot sauce, coconut aminos, onion powder, sea salt and mustard powder and give everything a quick stir. Secure the lid, close the pressure valve and press the Keep Warm/Cancel button. Then press the Pressure Cook/Manual button and press the +/- buttons until 5 minutes is displayed.

3. Allow the cooking cycle to complete, then quick release the pressure valve and remove the lid once safe to do so. Remove the turkey and drain off the liquid using a strainer. Set the turkey aside and return the liquid back to the Instant Pot.

4. Press the Keep Warm/Cancel button once more, then press the Sauté button and allow the sauce to reduce for about 5 minutes.

5. Serve by spooning the cooked turkey mixture into the romaine leaves and drizzling with the reserved sauce. Garnish with fresh chives or shredded carrots if desired.

CHICKEN MARSALA

+PALEO

★ MAKES: 4 SERVINGS ★
PREP TIME: 5 MINUTES
COOK TIME: 28 MINUTES

This recipe quickly became a family favorite at my house, even with my mushroom-loathing children. There is something about that Marsala wine that adds so much savory goodness—I think it could make any food delicious. This can quickly become a weeknight favorite and put boring chicken dishes behind you. You can even make this one 21DSD compliant by removing the cooking wine.

4 tbsp (60 ml) avocado oil

1 onion, chopped

20 oz (560 g) sliced mushrooms

1 tsp sea salt

1 tbsp (3 g) dried parsley

1 tsp garlic powder

½ tsp ground black pepper

¾ cup (180 ml) Marsala wine

2 lbs (900 g) chicken, chopped

½ cup (120 ml) Chicken Broth
(page 148)

1. Press the Sauté button on your Instant Pot, then pour in the avocado oil and allow it to sit for a moment. Introduce the onion and mushrooms to the hot oil and stir for about 10 minutes or until the mushrooms begin to brown.

2. Add in the sea salt, parsley, garlic powder, pepper and Marsala wine, then stir again to incorporate the seasonings and allow them to simmer for 2 minutes.

3. Add in the chopped chicken and pour in the chicken broth. Secure the lid to your Instant Pot and close the pressure valve. Press the Keep Warm/Cancel button then press the Pressure Cook/Manual button. Press the +/- buttons until 8 minutes is displayed.

4. Allow the cooking cycle to complete, then quick release the pressure valve and remove the lid once safe to do so. Use a slotted spoon or skimmer to remove the meat, onions and mushrooms, then press the Keep Warm/Cancel button and then the Sauté button.

5. Allow the sauce to simmer for about 5 to 8 minutes or until it reduces and thickens slightly. Serve over your choice of starch or veggie.

WHITE CHICKEN CHILI

+PALEO +21DSD +LOW CARB

+ MAKES: 6 SERVINGS +
PREP TIME: 5 MINUTES
COOK TIME: 17 MINUTES

I remember going to chili cook-offs in the past and wondering why in the world anyone would ever want to stray from REAL chili—the kind with beef and beans and lots of heat—for white chili. I admit that I used to turn up my nose, grab a bowl of the red stuff and snicker under my breath. I'm glad to say I've evolved since then, and can now appreciate what a great alternative white chili offers to traditional chili. I've even written a white chili recipe of my own! It's packed with flavor and swaps out tomatoes and beans for chicken and potatoes, making it a hearty but delightfully different choice.

2 tbsp (30 ml) avocado or olive oil

1 onion, diced

1 lb (450 g) chicken thighs

10 oz (285 g) cauliflower rice

2 medium Yukon Gold potatoes, peeled and chopped

1 clove garlic, minced

4 cups (960 ml) Chicken Broth (page 148)

¼ tsp white pepper

1 tsp sea salt

1 tsp chili powder

½ tsp cumin

Fresh cilantro (optional)

1. Press the Sauté button on your Instant Pot and drizzle in the oil. Add in the diced onion and cook for 5 minutes.

2. Press the Keep Warm/Cancel button, add in the remaining ingredients and secure the lid. Close the pressure valve, press the Pressure Cook/Manual button and use the +/- buttons to adjust the time until 12 minutes is displayed.

3. Allow the cooking cycle to complete and then quick release the pressure valve and remove the lid once safe to do. Use an immersion blender to briefly blend a couple areas of the bowl so that some of the ingredients are pureed but the rest remain chunky. Do this until your desired texture is reached.

4. Garnish with fresh cilantro if desired and serve warm.

CHICKEN TORTILLA SOUP

+PALEO +21DSD +LOW CARB +KETO

+ MAKES: 6 SERVINGS +
PREP TIME: 5 MINUTES
COOK TIME: 15 MINUTES

In Texas, you'll find as many versions of tortilla soup as there are wide open spaces. Whether creamy or broth-based, they usually call for masa flour and lots of cheese! This one packs in a punch of flavor, but uses clean, simple ingredients for a nutrient-dense meal.

6 cups (1.4 L) Chicken Broth (page 148)

1 lb (450 g) chicken breast

12 oz (340 g) fresh homemade or high quality store-bought salsa

1 tsp sea salt

1 tsp garlic powder

1 tsp onion powder

1 tsp chili powder

1 tsp cumin

1 tsp black pepper

1 cup (150 g) chopped carrots

1 onion, chopped

Fresh cilantro (optional)

Sliced avocado (optional)

1. Place all of the ingredients except the cilantro and sliced avocado into the stainless steel bowl of your Instant Pot and secure the lid. Close the pressure valve, press the Manual/Pressure Cook button and adjust the cook time to 15 minutes using your +/- buttons.

2. Allow the cooking cycle to complete and then quick release the pressure valve and remove the lid once safe to do so. Use two forks to shred the chicken.

3. Serve topped with fresh cilantro and sliced avocado if desired.

TOM KHA GAI

+PALEO +21DSD +LOW CARB +KETO

+ MAKES: 2 SERVINGS +
PREP TIME: 5 MINUTES
COOK TIME: 15 MINUTES

Who knew that such a complex set of flavors could be in such a simple dish? This has always been a restaurant favorite of mine, but when it's this easy to make at home, why go out? Plus, since it's pressure cooked, the flavors blend much more quickly, so there's no long wait to indulge.

1 lb (450 g) chicken thighs, cut into bite-size pieces

½ oz (14 g) dried chopped oyster mushrooms

1 (14-oz [385-ml]) can full-fat coconut milk

1 lime, juiced

1 cup (240 ml) Chicken Broth (page 148)

1 tbsp (4 g) chopped fresh lemongrass (or use 1 tsp dried if needed)

1 tbsp (15 ml) fish sauce

1 tbsp (14 g) fresh grated ginger

Sea salt

Fresh cilantro (optional)

1. Combine all of the ingredients except the salt and cilantro in the stainless steel bowl of your Instant Pot, then close the pressure valve and secure the lid. Press the Pressure Cook/Manual button and then use the +/- buttons until 15 minutes is displayed.

2. Allow the cooking cycle to complete and then quick release the pressure valve. Remove the lid once safe to do so and serve hot with sea salt and fresh cilantro to taste.

SHREDDED CAESAR CHICKEN

+PALEO +21DSD +LOW CARB +KETO

+ MAKES: 6 SERVINGS +
PREP TIME: 5 MINUTES
COOK TIME: 15 MINUTES

Have you ever made your own Caesar dressing? You should—it might be 87 times better than anything you can buy in the store, and chances are you have all of the ingredients you need at home already! Toss in some chicken and serve it on top of salad greens and you've got dinner in about 20 minutes, start to finish.

2 eggs

2 cloves garlic

½ tsp sea salt

½ tsp ground black pepper

1 tbsp (15 ml) apple cider vinegar

1 lemon, juiced

½ tsp mustard powder

½ tsp fish sauce

1 tbsp (14 g) ghee

1 cup (240 ml) avocado oil or light olive oil

2 lbs (900 g) boneless chicken breast

1 cup (240 ml) water

Romaine lettuce

1. In a mason jar, mix together the eggs, garlic, sea salt, pepper, apple cider vinegar, lemon juice, mustard powder, fish sauce and ghee.

2. Use an immersion blender to blend the ingredients well, then slowly drizzle in the avocado oil while shifting your immersion blender around to emulsify the dressing—it will make a little over 1 cup (240 ml). Set the dressing aside or refrigerate it.

3. Place the chicken in the stainless steel bowl of your Instant Pot and pour in the water. Season the uncooked chicken with additional sea salt and pepper. Secure the lid and close the pressure valve. Press the Pressure Cook/Manual button and then the +/- buttons until 15 minutes is displayed.

4. Allow the cooking cycle to complete, then quick release the pressure valve and remove the lid once safe to do so. Shred the chicken with two forks and serve it on a bed of romaine lettuce, drizzling the dressing as desired.

THANKSGIVING TURKEY BREAST

+PALEO +21DSD +AIP +LOW CARB +KETO

> **+ MAKES: 6 SERVINGS +**
> **PREP TIME: 5 MINUTES**
> **COOK TIME: 60 MINUTES**

I know, I know, this is not your traditional, fresh-out-of-the-oven roasted turkey. But it's so easy, tender and juicy, and it's quicker than quick! This turkey cooks with the push of a couple buttons and zero babysitting!

2 cups (480 ml) Chicken Broth (page 148) or Beef Broth (page 147)

3 lbs (1.3 kg) bone-in frozen turkey breast

2 tsp (12 g) sea salt

1 tsp onion powder

1 tsp garlic powder

½ tsp dried thyme

1 tsp dried parsley, plus more for garnish

2 tbsp (30 ml) olive oil, ghee or avocado oil

1. Pour in the broth and place the turkey directly into the pot, with no trivet. Add the seasonings onto the top of the breast and then drizzle with the oil. The skin is not going to crisp in the Instant Pot.

2. Secure the lid, close the pressure valve and then press the Manual/Pressure Cook button. Use the +/- buttons and adjust until 1 hour or 60 minutes is displayed.

3. Allow the cooking cycle to complete and then quick release the pressure valve and remove the lid once safe to do so. Carefully pour out the broth into a separate bowl and then remove the turkey.

4. Slice and serve, or if you desire, you can also transfer the cooked turkey into your oven in a baking dish and broil for a few minutes to help crisp the skin. This recipe pairs well with Cream-less Cream Gravy (page 167). Top with parsley if using.

5 MINUTE TACO MEAT

+PALEO +21DSD +LOW CARB

+ MAKES: 4 SERVINGS +
PREP TIME: 5 MINUTES
COOK TIME: 10 MINUTES

Sometimes, I get a craving, and if I don't figure out a way to satisfy that craving, I feel like I'm pregnant with octuplets during a national pickle shortage. Today, I needed nachos stat, and fortunately I had everything in house I needed to whip up this recipe. Crisis averted.

2 tbsp (30 ml) avocado or olive oil

1 lb (450 g) ground turkey

1 onion, diced

1 tbsp (9 g) minced garlic

½ cup (75 g) shredded carrots

½ tsp cumin

1 tsp chili powder

½ tsp sea salt

¼ tsp ground pepper

1 tsp onion powder

½ tsp ground chipotle powder

1½ cups (360 ml) tomato sauce

Cilantro (optional)

1. Press the Sauté button and add in your cooking oil, ground turkey, diced onion and garlic.

2. Sauté for around 5 minutes, breaking up the ingredients as they cook. The meat does not have to cook all the way through.

3. Add in the remaining ingredients, except the cilantro, give them a quick stir then secure the lid. Press the Keep Warm/Cancel button and then press the Pressure Cook/Manual button. Adjust the +/- buttons until 5 minutes is displayed.

4. Allow the cooking cycle to complete, then quick release the pressure valve and remove the lid once safe to do so. Use a slotted spoon to strain the meat mixture of excess juices. Serve it over cauliflower rice, in romaine hearts or on grain-free tortilla chips (which are not low carb or 21DSD). Garnish with cilantro, if desired.

OINK + BAA

A GREAT PULLED PORK that is slow smoked for hours, and so tender it just falls apart, can't be beat. But the unfortunate reality is that many of our best oven-baked pork attempts turn out as dried up hunks of meat that require lots of sauce and extra water to choke down.

One of the things I love about pressure cooking pork is that it seals in all the juices and keeps the meat tender, so your pork and lamb dishes come out just the way they would if they were made by the pros. This chapter is dedicated to all the less-than-savory pork dishes you were forced to consume over the years. Here's to you, overcooked pork and lamb—we promise to do better starting right now!

EGG ROLL MEATBALLS

+PALEO +21DSD +AIP +LOW CARB +KETO

+ MAKES: 4 SERVINGS +
PREP TIME: 5 MINUTES
COOK TIME: 10 MINUTES

After I developed this recipe, my husband said, "These are some of your best meatballs ever," and I knew it was a keeper. We are a big meatball-lovin' family, so that means lots of experimenting—I love when we nail a winner and everyone is happy!

1 lb (450 g) ground pork

1 cup (150 g) shredded carrots

½ onion, minced

1 tsp onion powder

1 tsp garlic powder

½ tsp ground ginger

½ tsp white pepper (omit for AIP)

2 tbsp (28 g) gelatin (not collagen)

⅓ cup (80 ml) olive or avocado oil

¾ cup (180 ml) Beef Broth (page 147)

¼ cup (60 ml) coconut aminos

Minced green onions, for garnish (optional)

1. Begin by mixing the pork, carrots, onion, onion powder, garlic powder, ground ginger and white pepper in a mixing bowl. Use your hands to mix the ingredients and then sprinkle the gelatin throughout the mixture, making sure to distribute it evenly so it doesn't clump.

2. Drizzle your cooking oil into the Instant Pot bowl and press the Sauté button. While the oil heats, form 1- to 2-inch (3- to 5-cm) meatballs with your meat mixture and then gently place them into the hot oil. You'll sauté them on all sides until they begin to brown, about 5 minutes. Shift them regularly or they may stick.

3. Once your meatballs are browned, press the Keep Warm/Cancel button and then pour in the broth and coconut aminos. Secure the lid and press the Pressure Cook/Manual button. Use the +/- buttons to adjust the time until 5 minutes is displayed.

4. Allow the cooking cycle to complete and then quick release the pressure valve and remove the lid once safe to do so. Use a slotted spoon or skimmer to remove the meatballs and set them aside. What's left in the Instant Pot is your sauce. Use an immersion blender to give it a quick once-over so that any bits left behind from the meatballs get blended in.

5. Some of the gelatin sneaks out of the meatballs during cooking and helps create the thickness of the sauce. It will congeal and harden as it cools, so you'll want to serve it warm, and if you make it ahead, you'll need to reheat the congealed sauce. Garnish with green onions, if desired.

DELUXE SAUSAGE PIZZA ZUCCHINI BOATS

+PALEO +21DSD +LOW CARB

* MAKES: 6 SERVINGS *
PREP TIME: 10 MINUTES
COOK TIME: 10 MINUTES

As a former cheese addict, the very idea of pizza is just dreamy to me. With this recipe, I've combined all of our favorite pizza flavors, but I've kept it dairy free so your body and skin will love it that much more!

3 medium zucchini squash, no longer than the diameter of your pressure cooker opening

1 tbsp (15 ml) avocado oil, olive oil or ghee

16 oz (450 g) pastured, nitrate-free breakfast sausage (uncooked)

1 small red onion, minced

2 oz (56 g) high-quality, nitrate-free pepperoni

24 oz (682 ml) no-sugar marinara sauce, divided

1 cup (240 ml) water

Sea salt and pepper to taste

Flat leaf parsley, for garnish (optional)

1. Slice the zucchinis length-wise and scoop out the flesh, making sure not to hollow them out too much, but removing all of the seeds. Set the zucchinis aside.

2. Drizzle the cooking oil into the stainless steel bowl of your Instant Pot and press the Sauté button. Add in your sausage, onion and pepperoni and cook until the sausage is cooked through, about 5 to 8 minutes. Shift the ingredients often so they do not burn.

3. Press the Keep Warm/Cancel button once the sausage is cooked through and carefully empty the contents of the stainless steel bowl into a mixing bowl. Stir in 12 ounces (341 ml) of the marinara sauce and divide the mixture among the 6 hollowed squash halves.

4. Remove and rinse your stainless steel Instant Pot bowl and place it back into the Instant Pot. Pour in the water and lower in the trivet/steaming tray, then carefully lower the zucchini halves onto it. You may carefully stack the zucchini halves if you need more room.

5. Secure the lid, press the Manual button and then press the +/- buttons until the display reads 5 minutes. Allow the cooking cycle to complete and then quick release the pressure valve and remove the lid once safe to do so. Carefully remove the cooked zucchini boats. Serve warm with the reserved 12 ounces (341 ml) of marinara sauce. Garnish with parsley, if desired.

MIXED CITRUS PULLED PORK

+PALEO

★ MAKES: 4 SERVINGS ★
PREP TIME: 5 MINUTES
COOK TIME: 45 MINUTES

You'll want to put this fail-proof recipe just about everywhere—on mixed greens, between slices of grain-free bread, rolled up in a paleo tortilla and most definitely straight into your mouth. Tons of flavor and hands-off cooking are a pair you can't pass up!

3 tbsp (45 ml) avocado oil or olive oil

1 onion, diced

2 jalapeños, seeded and diced

2 tbsp (18 g) minced garlic

2 tsp (12 g) sea salt

20 oz (570 g) crushed pineapple in water

3 tbsp (45 ml) apple cider vinegar

1 tbsp (15 ml) lemon juice

1 tsp onion powder

½ tsp paprika

½ tsp cumin

½ cup (120 ml) orange juice

2 lbs (900 g) pork roast

Fresh cilantro, for garnish (optional)

1. Press the Sauté button and drizzle in your cooking oil. Introduce your onion and jalapeños and cook for about 5 minutes, shifting the veggies periodically.

2. Put in the remaining ingredients, except the roast, and give them a quick stir before you place the roast on top. Spoon some of the mixture over the roast, press the Keep Warm/Cancel button and secure the lid. Seal the pressure valve and press the Pressure Cook/Manual button, then use the +/- buttons to adjust the time to 40 minutes.

3. Allow the cooking cycle to complete, then quick release the pressure valve and remove the lid once safe to do so. Shred the pork with two forks. Garnish with cilantro, if desired, before serving.

IRISH LAMB STEW

+PALEO +21DSD +AIP

MAKES: 6 SERVINGS
PREP TIME: 5 MINUTES
COOK TIME: 15 MINUTES

I'll never forget living overseas and making a quick hop to Ireland for a weekend—the food we experienced was so hearty, flavorful and memorable. I wanted this stew to be full of flavor like I remember, yet with ingredients that felt clean and safe for those of us who have to be careful with quality and sourcing. After my middle child went back for her third bowl, I knew I'd nailed it!

3 tbsp (45 ml) avocado oil or olive oil

1 large onion, diced

1 lb (450 g) lamb shoulder, cut into bite-size pieces

3 cups (720 ml) Beef Broth (page 147)

3 cups (450 g) peeled and chopped potato, white-fleshed sweet potato (for AIP or 21DSD)

1 cup (150 g) chopped carrots

1 tsp sea salt

¼ cup (60 ml) coconut aminos

1 heaping tsp garlic powder

1 heaping tsp onion powder

2 bay leaves

Pepper to taste (omit for AIP)

1. Press the Sauté button on your Instant Pot and drizzle in your cooking oil. Add in the onion and lamb, and sauté for about 5 minutes, shifting the meat so it is seared on all sides.

2. Add in the remaining ingredients and secure the lid. Close the pressure valve and press the Keep Warm/Cancel button. Press the Pressure Cook/Manual button and use your +/- buttons to adjust the time to 10 minutes.

3. Allow the cooking cycle to complete, then quick release the pressure valve and remove the lid once safe to do so. Remove the bay leaves. Use an immersion blender to quickly blend a couple sections of the stew to thicken the consistency. Aim for blending areas of potato instead of meat. Stir and then serve after your desired thickness is met.

TOMATILLO PORK

+PALEO +21DSD +LOW CARB +KETO

★ MAKES: 6 SERVINGS ★
PREP TIME: 5 MINUTES
COOK TIME: 14 MINUTES

I love that this dish is zesty without being overwhelmingly spicy, making it a great option for kids or those who don't do well with spice. Tomatillos are a great source of tangy and versatile flavor, and this dish is a perfect example of that!

2½ lbs (1.1 kg) pork loin, cut into bite-size pieces

3 tbsp (45 ml) avocado oil

1 onion, chopped

1 jalapeño, seeded

12 oz (340 g) peeled tomatillos

1½ cups (360 ml) Chicken Broth (page 148)

1 tsp sea salt

2 tsp (6 g) garlic powder

1 tsp onion powder

1 lime, juiced

1 tsp cumin

1 handful of cilantro, plus more for garnish

1. Place the pork loin pieces into the stainless steel bowl of your Instant Pot, then take the remainder of your ingredients and puree them in a blender.

2. Pour the sauce from the blender into the bowl with the pork. Secure the lid, close the pressure valve and press the Pressure Cook/Manual button, then press the +/- buttons and adjust until 14 minutes is displayed.

3. Allow the cooking cycle to complete, and then quick release the pressure valve and remove the lid once safe to do so. Give the pork a stir and serve topped with the rest of your fresh cilantro.

JAMAICAN JERK PORK LOIN

+PALEO +21DSD +LOW CARB

+ MAKES: 4 SERVINGS +
PREP TIME: 5 MINUTES
COOK TIME: 35 MINUTES

Get your taste buds ready; this one is going to take you for a flavor ride. It's a complex medley of flavors and is such a nice deviation from your typical pork loin. And if you like a little kick, this one is for you!

1 cup (240 ml) Chicken Broth (page 148)

¼ cup (60 ml) coconut aminos

1 onion, chopped

1 tbsp (9 g) minced garlic

1 tsp cinnamon

1 tsp dried thyme

1 tsp ground black pepper

1 tsp sea salt

¼ tsp ground nutmeg

¼ tsp allspice

¼ tsp ginger

¼ cup (60 ml) lime juice

1½ lb (675 g) pork loin

1 tsp cayenne pepper

1 tsp paprika

Mashed potatoes or mashed cauliflower, to serve (optional)

Fresh thyme sprigs, for garnish (optional)

1. Pour your chicken broth into the stainless steel bowl of your Instant Pot. In a blender or food processor, blend the coconut aminos, onion, garlic, cinnamon, thyme, pepper, sea salt, nutmeg, allspice, ginger and lime juice until smooth.

2. Place the pork loin in the broth, sprinkle the cayenne and paprika directly on top of the meat and then pour the puree over top. Secure the lid, close the pressure valve and press the Pressure Cook/Manual button, then adjust the +/- buttons until 30 minutes is displayed.

3. Allow the cooking cycle to complete, then quick release the pressure valve and remove the lid once safe to do so. Press the Keep Warm/Cancel button and then the Sauté button, allowing the gravy to reduce and thicken for about 5 minutes before serving.

4. Serve over mashed potatoes or mashed cauliflower and garnish with thyme if desired.

SAUSAGE + SPINACH SOUP

+PALEO +21DSD +AIP +LOW CARB +KETO

This is one of those "darn, I wish I had time to make a healthy meal" meals that you DO have time for, and it's likely all of the ingredients are already in your fridge! My husband told me I could make a soup like this every night and he'd be happy. I call that a win.

1 tbsp (14 g) ghee, avocado oil or olive oil

1 large onion, diced

1 lb (450 g) ground breakfast sausage (confirm spices are AIP compliant)

32 oz (910 ml) Chicken Broth (page 148) or Beef Broth (page 147)

1 tbsp (9 g) minced garlic

1 tsp sea salt

1 cup (150 g) chopped carrots

2 bay leaves

1 tsp onion powder

1 cup (30 g) fresh baby spinach, chopped

1. Begin by pressing the Sauté feature, then add your ghee or oil, onion and sausage to the Instant Pot. Break up the sausage and shift the onions for 5 minutes.

2. Add all of the remaining ingredients except for the spinach leaves. Secure the lid, close the pressure valve and press the cancel button, then press the Manual button. Use the +/- buttons to adjust the time until 5 minutes is displayed.

3. Allow the cooking cycle to complete, then quick release the pressure valve and remove the lid once safe to do so. Add in the spinach, give it a quick stir to wilt it and then serve right away or store in the fridge or freezer for later.

SOUTHWEST SPICY + SWEET CHILI

+PALEO +21DSD +LOW CARB

+ MAKES: 6 SERVINGS +
PREP TIME: 5 MINUTES
COOK TIME: 38 MINUTES

Chili fans, unite! If there is one meal that feels like the ultimate comfort food, it's chili. I love how different combinations of ingredients create such diverse flavors, and can be customized to accommodate your favorite blends. This recipe has hints of sweetness and spice, and is infused with a little Southwest flair.

1 lb (450 g) ground beef

1 lb (450 g) ground sausage

2 jalapeño peppers, seeded and diced

1 large sweet potato, diced

1 large onion, diced

26 oz (728 g) jarred crushed tomatoes

1 tsp sea salt

1 tsp cumin

2 tbsp (20 g) chili powder

1 tsp cayenne pepper

1 tbsp (9 g) minced garlic

3 tbsp (45 ml) coconut aminos

Fresh cilantro, diced avocado and sliced jalapeño, for garnish (optional)

1. Press the Sauté button on your Instant Pot and add your ground beef, sausage, jalapeños, sweet potato and onion. Sauté for about 8 minutes.

2. Pour in your crushed tomatoes and seasonings, secure the lid, close the pressure valve and press the Keep Warm/Cancel button. Press the Pressure Cook/Manual button and use the +/- buttons to adjust the time to 30 minutes.

3. Allow the cooking cycle to complete, then quick release the pressure valve and remove the lid once safe to do so. Serve topped with fresh cilantro, avocado and jalapeño, if desired.

SOUTHERN SAUSAGE + CABBAGE

+PALEO +21DSD +AIP +LOW CARB +KETO

★ MAKES: 4 SERVINGS ★
PREP TIME: 5 MINUTES
COOK TIME: 15 MINUTES

Growing up I always thought of cabbage as being really bland and boring. As an adult, though, I see the value in its sulfur-rich nutrition, so I wanted to make a really enjoyable cabbage dish. This Southern Sausage + Cabbage is full of flavor AND nutrition so you don't have to sacrifice one for the other, and it's such a quick meal to make.

3 tbsp (45 ml) avocado oil or olive oil

4 oz (112 g) raw bacon, chopped

1 onion, chopped

12 oz (340 g) sliced sausage, pastured kielbasa works great (use caution with seasonings for AIP)

1 head cabbage, sliced thin

1 cup (240 ml) Chicken Broth (page 148)

Sea salt

1. Press the Sauté button on your Instant Pot and add in the oil, allowing it to warm for a minute. Add in the bacon and onion and allow them to cook for 5 minutes, shifting them around periodically.

2. Add in your sausage, cabbage and chicken broth. Press the Keep Warm/Cancel button and then secure the lid and close the pressure valve. Press the Pressure Cook/Manual button and then the +/- buttons until it reads 10 minutes.

3. Allow the cooking cycle to complete and then quick release the pressure valve. Remove the lid once safe to do so and stir before serving. Add sea salt to taste.

MUSTARD CHIVE BONE-IN PORK CHOPS

+PALEO +21DSD +LOW CARB +KETO

> + MAKES: 4 SERVINGS +
> PREP TIME: 5 MINUTES
> COOK TIME: 30 MINUTES

One of the challenges of writing this book was not using a single thickener or sweetener, even Paleo-approved ones. I really wanted to stay committed to only using whole foods and ingredients that were easy to find at a mainstream grocery store. I'm really excited about the sauce in this recipe because though it took a little while to reduce, it's so delicious and savory on the pork chops.

3 tbsp (42 g) ghee, olive oil or avocado oil

4 bone-in pork chops

1 tbsp (9 g) minced garlic

2 cups (480 ml) Beef Broth (page 147), Chicken Broth (page 148) or pork broth

3 tbsp (50 g) Dijon mustard

2 tbsp (6 g) minced chives, plus more for garnish

¼ cup (60 g) coconut cream or the separated cream from a can of coconut milk

1. Press the Sauté button of your Instant Pot and spoon in the ghee or oil. Place your pork chops into the oil, searing them on each side for 2 minutes. You may have to sear just two at a time and switch them out. For the next step, you can stack them if needed.

2. After the pork chops are seared, press the Keep Warm/Cancel button and then add in the remaining ingredients except for the coconut cream. Secure the lid, close the pressure valve and press the Pressure Cook/Manual button. Use the +/- buttons to adjust the time until 15 minutes is displayed.

3. Once the cooking cycle completes, quick release the pressure valve and remove the lid once safe to do so. Remove the pork chops and set them aside, then press the Keep Warm/Cancel button once more.

4. Press the Sauté button and allow the sauce to simmer and reduce for 5 minutes or so, stirring to prevent burning. After a few minutes, add in the coconut cream and continue the simmer until the desired thickness of your sauce has been reached, about 10 minutes.

5. Serve the pork chops with the sauce and top with more fresh minced chives.

MOO

AS THE MOM OF THREE KIDS AND THE OWNER OF MULTIPLE BUSINESSES, I'll admit that ground beef recipes are my easy-peasy go-to for weeknight meals. In fact, there have been nights when I served seasoned ground beef with a steamed veggie and called it good. Real life looks like that.

But there's the other part of me that's like, look, you can do better than this. And the Instant Pot has been incredibly integral in making that true. So in this chapter, you'll find everything from Quick Barbacoa with a Kick (page 90) to Quick + Zesty Enchilada Soup (page 78) to Faux Pho (page 93). This chapter is dedicated to all those ground beef skillet meals that got the job done but were a little bit sad.

HAMBURGER SOUP

+PALEO +21DSD +AIP +LOW CARB

+ MAKES: 5 SERVINGS +
PREP TIME: 5 MINUTES
COOK TIME: 35 MINUTES

You know that meal that you keep on deck because everyone in the family is willing to eat it and nobody complains? That's this one. It's like a magical whip-it-up-serve-it-and-everyone's-happy meal. Sometimes you just need that one after a long week.

2 tbsp (30 ml) avocado oil

1 onion, diced

1 lb (450 g) ground beef

4 cups (960 ml) Beef Broth (page 147)

2 tsp (12 g) sea salt

1 tbsp (12 g) garlic powder

2 cups (300 g) chopped carrots

5 medium Yukon Gold potatoes, or white-fleshed sweet potatoes (for AIP or 21DSD)

Fresh rosemary, for garnish (optional)

1. Press the Sauté button on your Instant Pot, drizzle in the avocado oil and add the onion. Allow the onion to cook for about 5 minutes, shifting it around so that it doesn't burn, then add in the ground beef and break it up with a spatula.

2. Pour in the broth, add the seasonings, carrots and whole potatoes. Secure the lid and press the Keep Warm/Cancel button. Press the Pressure Cook/Manual button and use the +/- buttons to adjust the time until 30 minutes is displayed.

3. Allow the cooking cycle to complete and then quick release the pressure valve. Open the lid once safe to do so and use a potato masher to break up the potatoes until they are in small chunks. Serve warm and garnish with rosemary, if desired.

QUICK + ZESTY ENCHILADA SOUP

+PALEO +21DSD +LOW CARB

> **+ MAKES: 6 SERVINGS +**
> **PREP TIME: 5 MINUTES**
> **COOK TIME: 11 MINUTES**

As a native Texan, I'll tell you that this soup should theoretically be loaded down with corn masa, sour cream and more cheese than anyone could actually digest. However, as a clean eater, I'll tell you that though this soup tastes absolutely sinful it feels amazing in your body!

2 tbsp (28 g) ghee, olive oil or avocado oil

1 lb (450 g) ground beef

1 onion, diced

1 red bell pepper, diced

2 cups (480 ml) Chicken Broth (page 148)

14 oz (400 g) chopped cauliflower

1 (15-oz [426-ml]) jar of tomato sauce

1 tsp sea salt

1 tbsp (12 g) garlic powder

1 tsp onion powder

1 tsp cumin

½ tsp ground black pepper

1 tbsp (12 g) chili powder

1 tsp ground chipotle chili

Avocado (optional)

Fresh cilantro (optional)

1. Start by drizzling in your cooking fat or oil and pressing the Sauté button. Add in your ground beef and brown it, breaking it up while it cooks, for about 5 minutes or until no more pink remains.

2. Remove the cooked beef with a slotted spoon and set it aside, leaving behind the fat. Add in the onion and red bell pepper and sauté for about 3 minutes, then add in the remaining ingredients, except the avocado and cilantro, and press the Keep Warm/Cancel button.

3. Give the ingredients a quick stir, secure the lid, close the pressure valve and press the Pressure Cook/Manual button. Adjust the time with the +/- buttons until 3 minutes is displayed.

4. Allow the cooking cycle to complete, then quick release the pressure valve and remove the lid once safe to do so. Use an immersion blender to puree the soup base. Once you've reached your desired consistency, add back in the cooked ground beef.

5. Top with avocado, fresh cilantro or other desired toppings. Note that the grain-free tortilla chips featured in the photo are not 21DSD compliant or Low Carb.

MEXI MEATLOAF

+PALEO +21DSD +LOW CARB

+ MAKES: 5 SERVINGS +
PREP TIME: 10 MINUTES
COOK TIME: 35 MINUTES

I'm convinced that people who say they aren't "meatloaf people" just haven't met a meatloaf that's perfect for them yet. This magical little meatloaf might be the one, as it pairs zesty salsa and fresh cilantro with the perfect Mexican-inspired seasonings. It's certainly not your run-of-the-mill meatloaf; it's got attitude!

1 cup (240 ml) water

2 lbs (900 g) ground beef

1¼ cups (300 g) fire-roasted salsa, divided

1 tsp cumin

1 tsp garlic powder

1 tsp chili powder

1 tsp paprika

1 tsp onion powder

1 tsp sea salt

1 tsp ground black pepper

1 large yellow onion, diced

½ cup (105 g) mashed sweet potato, orange- or white-fleshed

2 tbsp (28 g) gelatin (not collagen)

Fresh cilantro (optional)

1. Pour the water into the stainless steel bowl of your Instant Pot, then combine all of the ingredients, except ¼ cup (60 g) of the salsa and the cilantro, in a bowl and mix them well by hand. Form a loaf with your meat mixture and press it together firmly. Spoon the remaining ¼ cup (60 g) of fire-roasted salsa on top of your meatloaf. Wrap it tightly in foil, then place it on a trivet in the Instant Pot.

2. Close the lid and the pressure valve and select the Pressure Cook/Manual button, using the +/- buttons to adjust the time until 35 minutes is displayed.

3. When the cook time has completed, quick release the pressure valve, open the lid once safe to do so and carefully remove your meatloaf. Serve with fresh cilantro sprigs if desired, and be sure to drizzle on my Queso Dip (page 155) for added cheesy deliciousness.

NO-BAKE SHEPHERD'S PIE

+PALEO +21DSD

+ MAKES: 4 SERVINGS +
PREP TIME: 5 MINUTES
COOK TIME: 15 MINUTES

This ultimate comfort food traditionally takes quite a bit of time and labor. I love that this version is so quick to pull together, even if you're getting three children into costumes single-handedly while making dinner and cleaning the house for guests. Surely I'm not the only one who's done that, right?

To make this 21DSD-compliant, please use the Minute Mashed Parsnip recipe (page 118) in lieu of mashed potatoes, and omit the peas in the photo.

MASHED POTATOES

¾ cup (180 ml) Beef Broth (page 147) or Chicken Broth (page 148)

¼ cup (56 g) ghee, olive oil or avocado oil

1 lb (450 g) medium white potatoes, like Yukon Gold or Russet, peeled and chopped

1 tsp sea salt

MEAT FILLING

2 tbsp (30 ml) avocado oil

1½ lb (675 g) ground beef

1 cup (150 g) finely chopped or shredded carrots

1 onion, chopped

½ tsp ground black pepper

1 tsp garlic powder

1 tsp sea salt

1 tsp onion powder

¼ cup (60 ml) coconut aminos

Fresh parsley to garnish (optional)

1. For the mashed potatoes, pour the broth and spoon the ghee or oil into the stainless steel bowl of your Instant Pot. Add in the chopped potatoes and secure the lid. Press the Pressure Cook/Manual button and then use the +/- buttons to adjust the time until 5 minutes is displayed.

2. Allow the cooking cycle to complete and then quick release the pressure valve and remove the lid once safe to do so. Transfer the potatoes and the remaining liquid to a mixing bowl.

3. For the meat filling, press the Sauté button and add in all of the meat filling ingredients. Shift the contents while the mixture cooks, about 10 minutes.

4. While the ground beef mixture cooks, use an immersion blender or fork to blend together the potato mixture and salt. An immersion blender will give you a smooth, creamy texture whereas a fork will give you a more textured result.

5. Once the meat mixture is cooked through and no pink is visible, press the Keep Warm/Cancel button and transfer the mixture into a casserole dish. Spoon the mashed potatoes on top of the meat mixture and serve, or you can pop it under the broiler in the oven for a minute or two if you'd prefer to crisp parts of the potato topping. Garnish with fresh parsley, if desired.

SWEDISH MEATBALLS + "CREAM" GRAVY

+PALEO +21DSD +AIP +LOW CARB

+ MAKES: 3 SERVINGS +
PREP TIME: 10 MINUTES
COOK TIME: 20 MINUTES

I am a meatball fanatic; I'm game for pretty much any variety of meatball. I love that they are great as appetizers, main courses and finger foods, and that they are bound to make both kids and grownups happy. This Swedish Meatball recipe tastes pretty sinful but is packed full of the good stuff your body loves!

GRAVY

2 cups (480 ml) Beef Broth (page 147)

¼ cup (60 ml) coconut aminos

½ tsp sea salt

½ tsp onion powder

½ tsp garlic powder

2 tbsp (28 g) ghee, olive oil or avocado oil

6 oz (112 g) white-fleshed sweet potato, coarsely chopped

MEATBALLS

1 lb (450 g) pastured ground beef

½ onion, minced

1 tbsp (14 g) gelatin (not collagen)

1 tsp onion powder

1 tsp garlic powder

1 tsp sea salt

1 tsp fresh or dried parsley, minced

2 tbsp (30 ml) coconut aminos

Parsley, for garnish (optional)

1. For the gravy, place all of the gravy ingredients in the stainless steel bowl of your Instant Pot, then secure the lid, close the pressure valve and press the Manual button. Press the +/- buttons until the display reads 5 minutes.

2. While the gravy cooks, assemble your meatballs by combining those ingredients, except the parsley, taking care to work the gelatin gradually into the meat so it does not clump and congeal.

3. Once the cooking cycle for the gravy is complete, quick release the pressure valve and remove the lid once safe to do so. Puree the gravy with an immersion blender. It may help to transfer it to a smaller bowl to blend, then return it to the stainless steel Instant Pot bowl.

4. Place the uncooked meatballs into the gravy, secure the lid, close the pressure valve and press the Keep Warm/Cancel button. Press the Pressure Cook/Manual button and then the +/- buttons until 10 minutes is displayed

5. Allow the cooking cycle to complete, then quick release the pressure valve and safely remove the lid. Remove the meatballs, quickly puree the gravy again with your immersion blender, then press the Keep Warm/Cancel button.

6. Press the Sauté button and allow the gravy to simmer for about 5 minutes or until it thickens to your desired consistency. Serve it on top of the meatballs and garnish with flat leaf parsley, if desired.

SPEEDY SLOPPY JOES

+PALEO

+ MAKES: 4 SERVINGS +
PREP TIME: 5 MINUTES
COOK TIME: 10 MINUTES

No need for a slow simmer for this gem. After a quick sauté, you'll need only a handful of minutes to get this sweet, zesty dish on the table.

2 tbsp (28 g) ghee, avocado oil or olive oil

1 onion, diced

1 lb (450 g) ground beef

1 cup (237 ml) tomato sauce

¼ cup (60 ml) coconut aminos

1 tsp paprika

1 tsp sea salt

1 tsp apple cider vinegar

½ tsp ground black pepper

4 pitted dates

4 oz (120 ml) Beef Broth (page 147)

Lettuce (optional)

Grain-free bread (optional)

Shredded carrots (optional)

1. Press the Sauté feature on your Instant Pot and spoon in the ghee or oil. Add the onions and ground beef and allow them to cook for about 5 minutes, breaking up the beef as they do.

2. Combine the remaining ingredients, except the lettuce, bread and carrots in a stand blender or use an immersion blender to puree them, then add them to the Instant Pot. Secure the lid, close the pressure valve and press the Keep Warm/Cancel button. Press the Pressure Cook/Manual button and then the +/- buttons until 5 minutes is displayed.

3. Allow the cooking cycle to complete, then quick release the pressure valve and remove the lid once safe to do so. Serve your Sloppy Joes on a bed of lettuce or a grain-free bread of your choice. Garnish with shredded carrots, if desired.

ASIAN-INSPIRED BEEF + BROCCOLI

+PALEO +21DSD +LOW CARB

+ MAKES: 4 SERVINGS +
PREP TIME: 5 MINUTES
COOK TIME: 22 MINUTES

This classic Chinese take-out dish is a long-time favorite, but once you've kicked gluten, grain and refined sugar, it can be extra tough to enjoy. But that's no longer the case, my friends—this recipe is as clean as they come!

2 tbsp (30 ml) sesame oil

2 tbsp (30 ml) olive oil or avocado oil

1 onion, diced

2 tbsp (18 g) minced garlic

1½ lbs (675 g) flank steak cut into bite-size pieces

1 tsp sea salt

¼ tsp white pepper

⅓ cup (80 ml) Beef Broth (page 147)

⅔ cup (160 ml) coconut aminos

20 oz (570 g) broccoli florets

1. Press the Sauté button and drizzle in your two cooking oils. Then add in the onion and allow it to soften for about 4 minutes. Add in the garlic and flank steak pieces and continue to sauté until the flank steak is browned on all sides, about 4 minutes.

2. Add in the remaining seasonings, broth and coconut aminos, stirring to combine. Lower in your steamer basket and place the broccoli into it. Press the Keep Warm/Cancel button, secure the lid and close the pressure valve.

3. Press the Pressure Cook/Manual button and then use the +/- buttons to adjust until 4 minutes is displayed. This will yield broccoli on the tender side. If you prefer more al dente broccoli, you'll want to adjust this by sautéing the beef longer and then pressure cooking for less time.

4. Once the cooking cycle is complete, release the pressure valve and remove the lid once safe to do so. If you want to thicken the sauce, simply remove the beef and broccoli with a slotted spoon, set them aside and then press the Keep Warm/Cancel button before pressing the Sauté button once more. Allow the sauce to simmer on the Sauté feature until the desired thickness is met, about 10 minutes or less.

5. Spoon the sauce over the finished beef and broccoli when it's plated.

QUICK BARBACOA WITH A KICK

+PALEO +21DSD +LOW CARB

+ MAKES: 6 SERVINGS +
PREP TIME: 5 MINUTES
COOK TIME: 62 MINUTES

There's a certain food chain that has me craving barbacoa so much I have it on speed dial. I love that tender, fall-apart, savory meat, and so I decided it was about time I made it at home—after all, I don't charge extra for guacamole.

2 tbsp (30 ml) olive oil or avocado oil

2 lbs (900g) beef brisket

1½ cups (360 ml) Beef Broth (page 147)

½ cup (120 ml) Adobo Sauce (page 164)

2 or 3 limes, juiced

Sea salt to taste

Paleo tortillas (optional, not 21DSD compliant or Low Carb)

Hearts of romaine (optional)

1. Press the Sauté button on your Instant Pot and then drizzle in your cooking oil. Place the brisket gently into the stainless steel bowl of your Instant Pot and sear it for approximately 2 minutes on each side.

2. Add in all the remaining ingredients, except the tortillas and romaine, press the Keep Warm/Cancel button, secure the lid and close the pressure valve. Press the Pressure Cook/Manual button and then use the +/- buttons to adjust the time until 1 hour or 60 minutes is displayed.

3. Allow the cooking cycle to complete and then quick release the pressure valve. Remove the lid once safe to do so and shred the beef with two forks. Serve it on Paleo tortillas or in hearts of romaine, if desired.

FAUX PHO

+PALEO +21DSD +LOW CARB +AIP +KETO

+ MAKES: 4 SERVINGS +
PREP TIME: 5 MINUTES
COOK TIME: 10 MINUTES

I was looking for pho recently in the middle of the cornfields we now live in—sorely missing the convenience of Washington, DC, where I could run down the street to pick up a hot steaming bowl of that Vietnamese magic—and I came up empty handed. I learned I would need to drive a solid forty minutes into the city to find any, and in that moment I decided I needed to make my own. While this isn't a truly traditional representation, it is a quick variation with ingredients you probably have right at home!

2 tbsp (30 ml) avocado oil

1 tsp sesame oil (omit for AIP)

16 oz (450 g) white button mushrooms, sliced

1 tbsp (15 ml) fish sauce

1 to 2 tsp (5 to 10 g) sea salt

½ tsp black pepper (omit for AIP)

1 tsp onion powder

1 tsp garlic powder

¼ cup (60 ml) coconut aminos

6 cups (1.4 L) Beef Broth (page 147)

1 onion, thinly sliced

Optional add-ins: 4 oz (112 g) thinly sliced cooked sirloin, fresh cilantro, lime juice, bean sprouts, jalapeño slices (omit for AIP), Sriracha or alternate chili sauce (omit for AIP), tapioca noodles (omit for 21DSD or Low Carb)

1. Drizzle the cooking oils into your Instant Pot and press the Sauté button. Add in the mushrooms and allow them to cook for about 5 minutes, shifting them so they don't stick or burn.

2. Add in the remaining seasonings, broth and onion. Press the Keep Warm/Cancel button and secure the lid. Close the pressure valve and press the Pressure Cook/Manual button, then use the +/- buttons to adjust the time until 5 minutes is displayed.

3. Allow the cooking cycle to complete and quick release the pressure valve. Remove the lid once safe to do so and serve with whichever optional add-ins you desire.

SPLASH

SOMETIMES THE SEAFOOD AISLE CAN BE INTIMIDATING. You see that giant fish, the scallops that you've never attempted to cook yourself and the shrimp that you aren't quite sure what to do with . . . so you walk on by. But seafood is such an amazing source of nutrients, and it's delicious too. So what's your beef with it? See what I did there?

The bottom line is that those of us who are intimidated by sea creatures just need reassurance that there are easy, thoughtless, go-to recipes out there for us to feel confident preparing. And thankfully there are! In these next pages, you'll find recipes like Cilantro Lime Shrimp Scampi + Spaghetti Squash (page 105), Creamy Crawfish Bisque (page 101) and even Crab-Stuffed Mushrooms (page 98)! This chapter is dedicated to all of the lonely seafood out there, desperately wishing to find a new home in your Instant Pot.

CAJUN SCALLOPS

+PALEO +21DSD +LOW CARB

+ MAKES: 4 SERVINGS +
PREP TIME: 5 MINUTES
COOK TIME: 12 MINUTES

I used to be a little nervous about making scallops at home, especially because once you've had good ones you know exactly how they should taste, and I for one did not want to mess that up. But since I wrote my first Instant Pot book, *Paleo Cooking with Your Instant Pot*®, I realized just how simple they are, and how quick too!

2 tbsp (28 g) ghee, olive oil or avocado oil

4 oz (112 g) of raw bacon, chopped

1 onion, diced

1 tsp paprika

1 tsp dry mustard

1 tsp cayenne pepper

¼ tsp black pepper

½ tsp cumin

1 tsp onion powder

1 tsp garlic powder

¼ tsp sea salt

½ tsp thyme

½ tsp oregano

1 lb (450 g) thawed or fresh jumbo scallops

1 cup (240 ml) Chicken Broth (page 148), Beef Broth (page 147), or Umami Broth (page 152)

Flat leaf parsley, for garnish (optional)

1. Press the Sauté feature on your Instant Pot and add in the cooking fat, bacon and onion. Allow the bacon and onion to cook for about 8 to 10 minutes, shifting them so they do not burn.

2. While the bacon and onion sauté, combine all of the seasonings in a small bowl and dredge the scallops in the seasonings on both sides.

3. Pour in the broth, press the Keep Warm/Cancel button and place the seasoned scallops into the broth. Secure the lid, close the pressure valve and press the Pressure Cook/Manual button, using the +/- buttons to adjust the time until 2 minutes is displayed.

4. Once the cooking cycle completes, quick release the pressure valve and remove the lid once safe to do so. Serve the scallops right away on top of the bacon and onion broth. Garnish with parsley, if desired.

CRAB-STUFFED MUSHROOMS

+PALEO +21DSD +LOW CARB +KETO

+ MAKES: 4 SERVINGS +
PREP TIME: 5 MINUTES
COOK TIME: 4 MINUTES

Whether you make these as appetizers or the main event, they are filling, nutritious and couldn't be any easier! I love the added kick from the ground chipotle powder!

6 oz (170 g) canned claw crabmeat

⅓ cup (70 g) mayonnaise

½ tsp onion powder

½ tsp garlic powder

½ tsp sea salt

½ tsp ground chipotle chile powder

2 tsp (9 g) gelatin (not collagen)

8 oz (225 g) button mushrooms, stemmed and cleaned

1 cup (240 ml) water

Chopped green onion, for garnish (optional)

1. Place all of the ingredients, except for the mushrooms, water and green onion, in a mixing bowl. Stir to combine well and then scoop 1 to 2 teaspoons (5 to 10 g) of the mixture into the hollowed mushroom caps.

2. Pour the water into the stainless steel bowl of your Instant Pot and lower in the trivet. Place the filled mushroom caps on the trivet. If you need more stability, you can place them inside a tempered glass baking dish or onto a sheet of foil you place on top of the trivet.

3. Secure the lid, close the pressure valve and press the Pressure Cook/Manual button. Use the +/- buttons and adjust the time until 4 minutes is displayed.

4. Once the cooking cycle completes, quick release the pressure valve and remove the lid once safe to do so. Carefully lift the cooked mushrooms out of the bowl and serve warm. Garnish with green onion, if desired.

CREAMY CRAWFISH BISQUE

+PALEO +21DSD +LOW CARB

+ MAKES: 4 SERVINGS +
PREP TIME: 5 MINUTES
COOK TIME: 15 MINUTES

Growing up in Houston, I always had access to the most delicious fresh Gulf seafood. My family spent many summers dining on Galveston's sea wall. This Creamy Crawfish Bisque reminds me of the seafood bisques we ate, made with heavy cream and thickened with flour, so hearty and amazing but certainly not allergen friendly. This one is of course made without dairy or thickeners of any kind so more people can enjoy this traditional Southern bisque.

1 onion, chopped

1 red bell pepper, chopped

4 tbsp (60 ml) avocado oil or light olive oil

1 tsp sea salt

1 tsp black pepper

½ cup (120 ml) sherry cooking wine (omit for 21DSD)

1 cup (240 ml) Chicken Broth (page 148)

2 tsp (10 g) crushed garlic

1 lb (450 g) crawfish tail meat (frozen)

1 bay leaf

½ tsp dried thyme

1 cup (240 ml) full-fat coconut milk

Fresh thyme or chives to garnish (optional)

1. Combine all of the ingredients except the coconut milk in the stainless steel bowl of your Instant Pot. Secure the lid and close the pressure valve, then press the Pressure Cook/Manual button. Press the +/- buttons until 15 minutes is displayed.

2. Allow the cooking cycle to complete, then quick release the pressure valve and remove the lid once safe to do so. Puree the mixture using an immersion blender or a vertical blender, then add the coconut milk and blend until smooth.

3. Serve right away with fresh thyme or chives to garnish, if desired.

HEARTY CLAM CHOWDER

+PALEO +21DSD +AIP +LOW CARB

> **+ MAKES: 4 SERVINGS +**
> **PREP TIME: 5 MINUTES**
> **COOK TIME: 12 MINUTES**

Clam chowder happens to be my husband's favorite, and sadly it's totally off limits when we dine out. Heavy cream and white flour make for some serious discomfort, so I've recreated this highly sought after soup with only the cleanest ingredients that will result in smiles only!

2 tbsp (30 ml) olive oil, avocado oil or ghee (not for AIP)

2 celery ribs, diced

1 large onion, diced

1 tbsp (9 g) minced garlic

¼ tsp white pepper

¼ tsp dried thyme

1 tsp sea salt

4 cups (960 ml) Chicken Broth (page 148)

2 medium white-fleshed sweet potatoes (use for AIP or 21DSD) or white potatoes, peeled and chopped

2 (6½-oz [184-g]) cans clams in clam juice

8 oz (225 g) crispy bacon, chopped

Chopped chives, for garnish (optional)

1. Spoon your oil into the stainless steel Instant Pot bowl and press the Sauté button, then introduce your celery, onion, garlic and seasonings. Cook until the veggies begin to soften, about 5 minutes, and then remove them from the bowl and set aside.

2. Press the Keep Warm/Cancel button and then pour in your broth and sweet potatoes. Secure the lid, close the pressure valve and press the Manual/Pressure Cook button, then use the +/- buttons until 5 minutes is displayed.

3. Allow the cooking cycle to complete, then quick release the pressure valve and remove the lid once safe to do so. Use an immersion blender to puree the soup—it should be nice and thick, but if it isn't the consistency you prefer, you'll be able to adjust this shortly.

4. Drain all but 1 tablespoon (15 ml) of the clam juice, then add the clams and the veggies into the Instant Pot.

5. Press the Sauté button and allow the soup to come to a simmer. If it's already your desired thickness, just simmer for 2 minutes so the clams heat through. If it's too thin, simmer a bit longer until it reduces to your desired thickness. And if it is too thick, add a bit more broth until your preferred thickness is met.

6. Top with the crisped bacon and chives, if desired, before serving.

CILANTRO LIME SHRIMP SCAMPI + SPAGHETTI SQUASH

+PALEO +21DSD +LOW CARB +AIP

+ MAKES: 2 SERVINGS +
PREP TIME: 5 MINUTES
COOK TIME: 6 MINUTES

The flavors in this dish are so robust you'll wonder why you haven't been making scampi like this all along. The ghee gives that rich, buttery flavor, and the lime, cilantro and garlic create an addicting flavor explosion.

¾ cup (165 g) ghee or avocado oil (for AIP)

1 lb (450 g) frozen, raw shelled shrimp

1 tsp sea salt

1 tbsp (9 g) minced garlic

1 handful cilantro (and more to garnish)

1 large lime, juiced

1 spaghetti squash, sliced in half horizontally

1. Spoon in your ghee or oil, add the shrimp and other ingredients and then place your spaghetti squash flesh-side down on top of the shrimp. Press the Pressure Cook/Manual button and then use the +/- buttons to adjust the cook time to 6 minutes.

2. Allow the cooking cycle to complete, then quick release the pressure valve and remove the lid once safe to do so. Carefully remove the hot spaghetti squash and scoop out the seeds. Then scoop out the spaghetti squash "noodles" and place them aside.

3. Add the cooked shrimp and melted ghee on top of the spaghetti squash "noodles" and top with extra fresh cilantro for serving.

SEAFOOD MEDLEY SPREAD

+PALEO +21DSD +LOW CARB +AIP

+ MAKES: 10 SERVINGS +
PREP TIME: 5 MINUTES
COOK TIME: 8 MINUTES

Seafood in the Instant Pot can pose a challenge sometimes. You don't want to overcook delicate fish or shrimp, but they're such a great source of nutrition you want to make sure they get a spot on your menu. This recipe started out as another concept altogether, and while that idea failed, it came together beautifully as a spread for veggies or grain-free crackers. I actually had trouble not eating it all before I photographed it, and the kids loved it too!

1 cup (240 ml) water

2 large carrots

12 oz (340 g) white-fleshed sweet potato, peeled and coarsely chopped

4 oz (112 g) canned albacore tuna, drained

2 oz (56 g) canned salmon, drained

4½ oz (126 g) canned 100% crabmeat, drained

1 tsp sea salt

1 tsp onion powder

1 tsp garlic powder

2 tbsp (28 g) gelatin (not collagen)

Veggies (optional)

Parsley (optional)

1. Pour the water into the stainless steel bowl of your Instant Pot, then add your carrots and sweet potato pieces directly into the water.

2. Secure the lid, close the pressure valve and press the Pressure Cook/Manual button. Use the +/- buttons to adjust the time until 8 minutes is displayed.

3. Allow the cooking cycle to complete, then quick release the pressure valve. Scoop out the vegetables with a slotted spoon or skimmer and add them to a bowl with the remainder of the ingredients, except for the parsley and serving vegetables.

4. Mix and mash the ingredients until they are well combined, then spoon them onto a sheet of foil. Wrap the foil around the spread like a meatloaf and lower it into your trivet, adding more water if needed to equal around 1 cup (240 ml).

5. Secure the lid once more, press the Keep Warm/Cancel button, close the pressure valve and press the Pressure Cook/Manual button. Use the +/- buttons and adjust the time until 0 minutes is displayed. Yes, zero minutes. It will take a few minutes to come to pressure and that will complete the cycle.

6. Quick release the pressure valve, then remove the lid once safe to do so. Carefully remove the foil-wrapped spread then scoop it into a serving bowl. Serve warm or chilled with sliced vegetables. Garnish with parsley if desired.

RED CURRY COD

+PALEO +21DSD +LOW CARB

+ MAKES: 6 SERVINGS +
PREP TIME: 2 MINUTES
COOK TIME: 4 MINUTES

I had literally only a handful of minutes to throw dinner together when I made this. I need to mention that I also have a husband who doesn't love tomato-based things, and three kids who don't necessarily gravitate towards ethnic cuisines. That said, this was so good it was approved by everyone at the table! And it's so fast, even with frozen fish, which was just as big a win for me!

1 lb (450 g) frozen cod fillets

½ cup (120 ml) Chicken Broth (page 148), Beef Broth (page 147) or fish broth

1 (15-oz [440-ml]) can full-fat coconut milk

1 (15-oz [440-g]) can tomato sauce

2 tbsp (28 g) red curry paste

1 cup (150 g) shredded carrots

1 onion, diced

1 tsp onion powder

3 tbsp (42 g) garlic, minced

Sea salt to taste

Cauliflower rice (optional)

Parsley or cilantro (optional)

1. Combine all of the ingredients except for the parsley and cauliflower rice in the stainless steel bowl of your Instant Pot. Give them a quick stir and then secure the lid, close the pressure valve and press the Pressure Cook/Manual button. Press the +/- buttons until 4 minutes is displayed.

2. Allow the cooking cycle to complete, then quick release the pressure valve and remove the lid once safe to do so.

3. Stir once more, gently breaking up the cooked fish fillets, and then serve the curry on top of cauliflower rice and garnish it with the parsley if desired.

ROUX-LESS GUMBO

+PALEO +21DSD +LOW CARB

+ MAKES: 6 SERVINGS +
PREP TIME: 5 MINUTES
COOK TIME: 16 MINUTES

While it may be sinful in The Big Easy, this roux-less gumbo is jam-packed with flavor, spice and everything nice. Plus, who has time to babysit a roux these days? Just sauté a few ingredients, press a few buttons and you've got gumbo in an instant.

¼ cup (60 ml) olive oil or avocado oil

12 oz (340 g) sliced sausage, like kielbasa

6 oz (170 g) frozen sliced okra

1 onion, diced

½ green bell pepper, chopped

1 lb (450 g) raw, frozen peeled shrimp

4 cups (960 ml) Chicken broth (page 148), Beef Broth (page 147), Vegetable Broth (page 151) or seafood broth

2 bay leaves

⅔ cup (160 g) tomato sauce

¼ tsp black pepper

½ tsp cayenne pepper

1 tsp sea salt

1 tsp garlic powder

Cauliflower rice, to serve (optional)

Flat leaf parsley, for garnish (optional)

1. Press the Sauté button and drizzle in your cooking oil. Introduce the sausage, okra, onion and bell pepper to the oil and sauté for 8 minutes, shifting the contents so they do not burn.

2. Add in the remaining ingredients, except the cauliflower rice, and press the Keep Warm/Cancel button. Secure the lid. Press the Pressure Cook/Manual button and use the +/- buttons to adjust the time until 8 minutes is displayed.

3. Allow the cooking cycle to complete and then quick release the pressure valve and remove the lid once safe to do so. Serve with cauliflower rice and garnish with parsley, if desired.

CHILI LIME SALMON

+PALEO +21DSD +LOW CARB

+ MAKES: 3 SERVINGS +
PREP TIME: 5 MINUTES
COOK TIME: 3 MINUTES

Salmon is a great fish option because it is so versatile, adapting to whatever flavors you toss at it. This recipe uses zesty spices and tart lime for a whole-bodied flavor profile. If you want to kick up the spice, you can increase the cumin, chipotle powder and sea salt, and if you want to cook frozen fish adjust the cook time to 5 or 6 minutes.

1 cup (240 ml) water

¼ cup (56 g) ghee, avocado oil or olive oil

1 tsp sea salt

1 tsp onion powder

1 tsp garlic powder

½ tsp cumin

½ tsp ground chipotle chili powder

1 lime, juiced

2 pitted dates

16 oz (450 g) salmon

Fresh cilantro (optional)

1. Pour the water into the stainless steel bowl of your Instant Pot. Lower in the trivet.

2. Blend all of the remaining ingredients, except for the salmon and cilantro, together in a food processor or with an immersion blender.

3. Spread the puree onto the salmon and wrap it loosely in parchment paper or foil. Lower it onto the trivet, secure the lid and close the pressure valve. Press the Pressure Cook/Manual button and use the +/- buttons to adjust the time until 3 minutes is displayed.

4. Allow the cooking cycle to complete, then quick release the pressure valve and remove the lid once safe to do so. Top with fresh cilantro, if desired, and serve.

SPROUT

IF THERE'S ONE THING WE CAN AGREE ON, it's that veggies are one of the most important things you can consume. And the sad truth is that most of us are not getting nearly enough of these micronutrients daily without having to supplement with multivitamins or other nutritional aids.

This chapter is dedicated to all the lonely vegetables out there just waiting to take up residence in your body. You'll find plant-based recipes like Quick-Pickled Onions (page 138), Turmeric Tomato Detox Soup (page 117) and Popeye Soup (page 126), which will all leave you feeling well fed and nourished!

TURMERIC TOMATO DETOX SOUP

+PALEO +21DSD +LOW CARB +VEGETARIAN

+ MAKES: 6 SERVINGS +
PREP TIME: 5 MINUTES
COOK TIME: 17 MINUTES

What I love most about a good tomato soup is that it's great to eat year-round; it's warm and comforting, yet not too heavy for a summer day. This one sneaks in liver-essential detox aids like turmeric and cilantro, so not only will it soothe your soul, it can do great things for your whole system!

4 tbsp (56 g) ghee, avocado oil or olive oil

1 large onion, chopped

3 large carrots, chopped

28 oz (784 g) crushed tomatoes

1 tsp garlic, minced

1 tsp onion powder

1 tsp sea salt

½ tsp ground black pepper

3 tsp (9 g) ground turmeric

2½ cups (600 ml) Vegetable Broth (page 151)

1 cup (240 ml) coconut milk

½ cup chopped cilantro

Pepitas (optional)

Nutritional yeast (optional)

1. Press the Sauté button and spoon the ghee or oil into the stainless steel bowl of your Instant Pot. Add the onion and carrots and allow them to sauté for about 5 minutes, or until they begin to soften.

2. Add in all remaining ingredients except the coconut milk. Secure the lid, press the Keep Warm/Cancel button and seal the pressure valve. Press the Pressure Cook/Manual button and use the +/- buttons to adjust the time until 12 minutes is displayed.

3. Allow the cooking cycle to complete, then quick release the pressure valve and remove the lid once safe to do so. Pour in the coconut milk and use an immersion blender to puree until the texture is uniform and smooth. If you don't have an immersion blender, you can carefully transfer the hot contents to a vertical blender.

4. Garnish with chopped cilantro before serving and add pepitas or nutritional yeast, if desired.

MINUTE MASHED PARSNIPS

+PALEO +LOW CARB +21DSD +AIP

| MAKES: 4 SERVINGS |
| PREP TIME: 5 MINUTES |
| COOK TIME: 7 MINUTES |

Mashed potatoes are always a comforting favorite, but if you are sensitive to nightshades or are eating Low Carb, potatoes are typically off the list. These mashed parsnips are so creamy and delicious you'll forget they aren't packed with carbs or heavy cream.

1 cup (240 ml) water

1½ lbs (675 g) parsnips, peeled and trimmed

½ cup (120 ml) canned coconut milk

¼ cup (60 ml) avocado oil or olive oil

1 tsp sea salt

½ tsp black pepper (omit for AIP)

½ tsp garlic powder

Fresh chives (optional)

Ghee (optional)

1. Pour the water into the stainless steel Instant Pot bowl. Add in the parsnips, secure the lid, and close off the pressure valve. Press the Steam button then press the +/- buttons until 7 minutes is displayed.

2. Allow the cooking cycle to complete, then quick release the pressure valve and remove the lid once safe to do so. Drain the water and transfer the parsnips to a mixing bowl.

3. Add in the remaining ingredients, except the chives and ghee, and then use an immersion blender to blend until creamy.

4. Top with fresh chives and melted ghee, if desired.

CRISPY GHEE-LICIOUS SMASHED POTATOES

+PALEO +21DSD

+ MAKES: 4 SERVINGS +
PREP TIME: 5 MINUTES
COOK TIME: 10 MINUTES

Let me introduce you to your new favorite way to eat potatoes. You can have crispy smashed potatoes in a little over 10 minutes, without ever heating up your oven! Seriously, it's that simple and that delicious.

1 cup (240 ml) water

24 oz (672 g) baby potatoes (e.g., fingerling, Dutch, rainbow)

¼ cup (56 g) ghee

¼ cup (60 ml) olive oil

Sea salt and black pepper, to taste

1. Pour the water into the stainless steel bowl of your Instant Pot and lower in your trivet/steamer tray.

2. Place the potatoes on the trivet. Secure the lid, close the pressure valve and press the Pressure Cook/Manual button. Use the +/- buttons until 5 minutes is displayed.

3. Allow the cooking cycle to complete. Quick release the pressure valve and remove the lid once safe to do so. Carefully remove the potatoes and trivet and pour out the water. Press the Keep Warm/Cancel button and then press the Sauté button.

4. Spoon in both cooking fats and then lower the potatoes back in, directly into the oil. Use a potato masher or large spoon to smash each potato so that it is slightly flattened. Allow potatoes to cook on each side for about 5 minutes, or until they begin to crisp.

5. Press the Keep Warm/Cancel button again and carefully remove the hot potatoes. Season with salt and pepper and serve.

OLD COUNTRY BEET BORSHT

+PALEO +21DSD +LOW CARB +AIP +VEGETARIAN

> + MAKES: 4 SERVINGS +
> PREP TIME: 5 MINUTES
> COOK TIME: 15 MINUTES

Borsht is one of the prettiest soups around, but it doesn't stop there! This soup gets its gorgeous color from its nutrient-dense beets, which are known for their vitamin C, manganese, potassium and folate. So while you dine in style, you can also feel fancy on the inside.

3 tbsp (42 g) ghee, olive oil or avocado oil

3 small beets, chopped

1 large onion, peeled and chopped

2 large carrots, chopped

4 cups (960 ml) Beef Broth (page 147) or Vegetable Broth (page 151)

1 tsp sea salt, plus more if desired

1 tsp garlic powder

Coconut cream (optional)

Micro greens (optional)

1. Spoon the ghee or oil into the stainless steel bowl of your Instant Pot and press the Sauté button. Add the beets, onion and carrots and sauté for 5 minutes, shifting the veggies so they don't burn.

2. Press the Keep Warm/Cancel button and add the broth. Secure the lid and press the Manual button, then press the +/- buttons until 10 minutes is displayed.

3. Allow the cooking time to complete, then quick release the pressure valve and remove the lid when safe to do so. Puree the cooked soup with an immersion blender or by transferring the contents to a vertical blender, then season as needed and garnish with coconut cream and micro greens, if desired.

INDIAN-INSPIRED "BUTTER" CAULIFLOWER

+PALEO +21DSD +VEGETARIAN +LOW CARB

★ MAKES: 3 SERVINGS ★
PREP TIME: 5 MINUTES
COOK TIME: 6 MINUTE

One of my favorite Indian dishes is butter chicken, with its layers of spice and creaminess. I decided it would be fun to make that same dish veggie-style so that even more of us could enjoy it!

4 tbsp (56 g) ghee

1 onion, diced

16 oz (450 g) chopped cauliflower

1 tbsp (9 g) garlic, minced

2 tsp (6 g) garam masala

½ tsp chili powder

½ tsp cumin

1 cup (245 g) tomato sauce

1 cup (240 g) coconut cream

Fresh cilantro, chopped (optional)

1. Start by pressing the Sauté button on your Instant Pot and spooning in your ghee. Introduce your diced onion to the hot ghee and sauté for 5 minutes, shifting the onion so it does not burn.

2. Press the Keep Warm/Cancel button, and add all the remaining ingredients except for the cilantro. Give them a quick stir before securing the lid and closing off the pressure valve. Press the Pressure Cook/Manual button and then use the +/- buttons to adjust the time until 1 minute is displayed.

3. Allow the cooking cycle to complete, then quick release the pressure valve and remove the lid once safe to do so. Serve warm and garnish with fresh cilantro.

NOTE: Coconut cream is the result of separated canned coconut milk upon refrigeration. Some stores carry canned coconut cream as well.

POPEYE SOUP

+PALEO +21DSD +LOW CARB +AIP

MAKES: 6 SERVINGS
PREP TIME: 5 MINUTES
COOK TIME: 15 MINUTES

This beauty may not be the belle of the ball, but don't overlook it just yet—it's nutrient dense and tastes amazing too. It is power packed with all your favorite vitamins, and it's so delicious the kids might just ask for seconds!

2 tbsp (28 g) ghee

1 large onion, coarsely chopped

1 large head of cauliflower, coarsely chopped (florets only)

2 oz (56 g) cilantro

2 cups (340 g) broccoli, coarsely chopped

2 cups (60 g) baby spinach leaves

5 cups (1.2 L) Chicken Broth (page 148)

1 cup (240 ml) coconut milk

1 tbsp (9 g) garlic, chopped

3 tsp (18 g) sea salt

2 tsp (10 ml) onion powder

Black pepper to taste (omit for AIP)

Fresh herbs (optional)

Chopped cilantro and red onion (optional)

1. Spoon the ghee into the stainless steel bowl of your Instant Pot and press the Sauté button. Introduce the onion to the ghee and sauté for 10 minutes, stirring occasionally so the onion does not burn.

2. Place all of the remaining ingredients except the fresh herbs into the bowl, press the Keep Warm/Cancel button and secure the lid. Close off the pressure valve and then press the Pressure Cook/Manual button. Adjust the time with the +/- buttons until the display reads 5 minutes.

3. Allow the cooking cycle to complete and then release the pressure valve. Remove the lid once safe to do so and use an immersion blender to completely puree all of the ingredients. The soup should be thick and creamy. If you want it thinner, you can add more broth until the desired consistency is reached.

4. Serve topped with fresh herbs, chopped cilantro and red onion, if desired.

LOADED EGG DROP SOUP

+PALEO +21DSD +LOW CARB +VEGETARIAN

+ MAKES: 4 SERVINGS +
PREP TIME: 5 MINUTES
COOK TIME: 15 MINUTES

What I love most about this soup is its ability to be filling yet not too heavy. That makes it a perfect soup for any season, and you probably already have all of the ingredients on hand too!

4 tbsp (56 g) ghee

1 tsp sesame oil

1 onion, diced

10 oz (285 g) button mushrooms, sliced

1 cup (150 g) carrots, chopped

1 tbsp (9 g) garlic, minced

1 tsp sea salt

1 tsp onion powder

4 cups (960 ml) Chicken Broth (page 148) or Vegetable Broth (page 151)

¼ cup (60 ml) coconut aminos

2 eggs, whisked

Green onion, minced (optional)

1. Spoon your ghee and sesame oil into the stainless steel bowl of your Instant Pot. Then add in your onion, mushrooms and carrots and press the Sauté button. Sauté the veggies for 10 minutes, shifting them along the way so they do not stick or burn.

2. Add in all of the remaining ingredients, except for the eggs and green onion, press the Keep Warm/Cancel button and then secure the lid and close the pressure valve. Press the Pressure Cook/Manual button and then use the +/- buttons to adjust the time until 5 minutes is displayed.

3. Allow the cooking cycle to complete, then quick release the pressure valve and remove the lid once safe to do so. Press the Keep Warm/Cancel button once more and then press the Sauté button. Allow the soup to come to a simmer and slowly add in the eggs, which will cook as they hit the boiling soup. Stir the soup gently as you add in the egg and then serve hot, topped with minced green onion, if desired.

QUICKEST FRENCH ONION SOUP

+PALEO +21DSD +LOW CARB +AIP +VEGETARIAN +KETO

+ MAKES: 4 SERVINGS +
PREP TIME: 5 MINUTES
COOK TIME: 25 MINUTES

Slow-cooked French onion soup is the best when it fills your home with that fragrant aroma of caramelized onions and savory broth. But the wait time for that slow-cooked goodness is a lot less fun. This recipe quickly caramelizes the onions and then, with one quick pressure cook cycle, you're ready to dig in!

½ cup (112 g) ghee (avoid for AIP), olive oil or avocado oil

3 medium onions, thinly sliced

1 tsp sea salt, plus more to taste

1 tbsp (9 g) minced garlic

2 sprigs fresh thyme, plus more for garnish

3 bay leaves

½ tsp ground black pepper (omit for AIP)

8 cups (1.9 L) Beef Broth (page 147) or Umami broth (page 152) or Vegetable Broth (page 151)

1. Press the Sauté button and drizzle in your cooking fat. Add the onions, shifting them every so often for about 15 minutes or until they begin to brown and caramelize.

2. Add in the remaining ingredients, except the garnishing thyme, press the Keep Warm/Cancel button and then secure the lid. Close the pressure valve and press the Pressure Cook/Manual button, adjusting the time with the +/- button until it reads 10 minutes.

3. Allow the cooking cycle to complete and then quick release the pressure valve and remove the lid once safe to do so. Remove the bay leaves. Add a bit more sea salt and fresh thyme as desired before serving.

BUTTERED CARROT BISQUE

+PALEO +21DSD +AIP +VEGETARIAN

+ MAKES: 4 SERVINGS +
PREP TIME: 5 MINUTES
COOK TIME: 13 MINUTES

I surprised myself with this recipe. I am not a huge fan of certain soups, like gazpacho and pureed veggie soups; I know there are great ones, but I'm typically the kind of girl that likes warm, hearty soup with meat and chunks of vegetables. However, this soup is a real treat. It's smooth, creamy and buttery, and it tastes like I should be sneaking guilty bites when in fact it only takes a handful of 100 percent whole food ingredients.

4 tbsp (56 g) ghee, or olive oil (for AIP)

1 tbsp (9 g) garlic, minced

1 onion, diced

1 lb (450 g) carrots

2 cups (480 ml) Vegetable Broth (page 151)

1 tsp sea salt

Cilantro or flat leaf parsley (optional)

1. Press the Sauté button and spoon the ghee into the stainless steel bowl of your Instant Pot. Add in the garlic and onion and cook for around 5 minutes, shifting the contents so they do not burn.

2. Add in the remaining ingredients, except the herbs, press the Keep Warm/Cancel button, close the lid and secure the pressure valve. Press the Pressure Cook/Manual button and use the +/- buttons to adjust the time until 8 minutes is displayed.

3. Allow the cooking cycle to complete, quick release the pressure valve and remove the lid once safe to do so. Use an immersion blender to puree the soup and then serve hot, topped with cilantro or fresh parsley, if desired.

DAIRY-FREE BROCCOLI "CHEESE" SOUP

+PALEO +21DSD +AIP +LOW CARB +VEGETARIAN

**+ MAKES: 4 SERVINGS +
PREP TIME: 2 MINUTES
COOK TIME: 8 MINUTES**

Yes! This recipe hits all the right spots: tons of veggies, whole food–based and safe for just about anyone looking to fill their bodies up with the good stuff. It's like a multi-vitamin in a soup bowl!

1 large peeled sweet potato, chopped

2 celery ribs, diced

¼ cup (56 g) ghee, avocado oil or olive oil

4 cups (960 ml) Vegetable Broth (page 151)

1 large onion, diced

1 tsp sea salt

1 tbsp (9 g) garlic, minced

1 tsp onion powder

12 oz (340 g) chopped broccoli

3 tbsp (30 g) nutritional yeast

¼ cup (60 ml) coconut cream (optional)

Fresh chives, pumpkin or sunflower seeds, or dairy-free Paleo "cheese" (not 21DSD) (optional)

1. Combine the sweet potato, celery, cooking fat, broth and onion in the stainless steel bowl of your Instant Pot. Give them a quick stir, then secure the lid and close the pressure valve. Press the Pressure Cook/Manual button and use the +/- buttons to adjust the time until 5 minutes is displayed.

2. Allow the cooking cycle to complete, then quick release the pressure valve and remove the lid once safe to do so. Use an immersion blender to puree the mixture until it's creamy.

3. Add in the seasonings, chopped broccoli, nutritional yeast and coconut cream. Secure the lid, close the pressure valve once more and press the Pressure Cook/Manual button. Use the +/- buttons to adjust the time until 3 minutes is displayed.

4. Allow the cooking cycle to complete, then quick release the pressure valve, removing the lid once safe to do so. Serve topped with fresh herbs, seeds or Paleo "cheese," if desired.

CREAMY ASPARAGUS SOUP

+PALEO +21DSD +AIP +LOW CARB +VEGETARIAN +KETO

+ **MAKES: 4 SERVINGS** +
PREP TIME: 2 MINUTES
COOK TIME: 15 MINUTES

My first assignment as a military spouse was in Germany. Among the many other memories I have of that time, I vividly recall that when a particular food was in season, you would find it everywhere! *Spargel* is the German word for asparagus, and from February to June you'd find it sautéed, roasted, in soups and quiches and so on in almost every restaurant you came across. This soup reminds me of those days in the best way!

1 bunch asparagus, trimmed

1 cup (240 ml) Vegetable Broth (page 151)

¼ cup (56 g) ghee, or avocado oil (for AIP)

1 tsp sea salt

1 tsp lemon juice

1 cup (240 ml) full-fat canned coconut milk

1 onion, diced

1 tbsp minced garlic

Micro greens, for garnish (optional)

1. Place all of the ingredients in the stainless steel bowl of your Instant Pot and give them a quick stir. Secure the lid, close the pressure valve and press the Pressure Cook/Manual button. Use the +/- buttons to adjust the time until 15 minutes is displayed.

2. Allow the cooking cycle to complete, then quick release the pressure valve, removing the lid once safe to do so. Use an immersion blender to puree the soup, or you can transfer the contents carefully to a vertical blender and puree that way.

3. Garnish with micro greens, if desired.

QUICK-PICKLED ONIONS

+PALEO +21DSD +LOW CARB +AIP +VEGETARIAN

+ MAKES: 4 SERVINGS +
PREP TIME: 2 MINUTES
COOK TIME: 2 MINUTES

Traditional pickled onions are delicious, but they take a long time to "get ready." These onions are great because after a quick swim in the Instant Pot and a cool down in the fridge they're yours for the taking!

1 red onion, sliced into thin rings

⅔ cup (160 ml) apple cider vinegar

⅓ cup (80 ml) water

1 clove garlic

1 tsp sea salt

1. Combine all of the ingredients in your Instant Pot bowl and secure the lid. Press the Pressure Cook/Manual button and then use the +/- buttons to adjust the time until 2 minutes is displayed.

2. Allow the cooking cycle to complete, then quick release the pressure valve and remove the lid once safe to do so. Transfer the onions and a little bit of the liquid to a glass jar. Place it in the fridge to chill for an hour or until cold.

3. Serve on your favorite salad or alongside a protein.

HOT MINUTE SPINACH + ARTICHOKE DIP

+PALEO +21DSD +LOW CARB +AIP +VEGETARIAN

> ✦ **MAKES: 8 SERVINGS** ✦
> **PREP TIME: 5 MINUTES**
> **COOK TIME: 15 MINUTES**

There is a spinach and artichoke dip from my childhood that I can still taste when I close my eyes and imagine it. It was the perfect blend of saltiness, creaminess and gooeyness that all added up to the perfect dip. While I won't ever forget it, I also won't be indulging in it these days, so I wrote this recipe to fill that void and deliver a nice big heap of veggies too!

1 cup (240 ml) water

1 small white-fleshed sweet potato (needs to yield ½ cup [105 g] mashed)

1½ cups (360 ml) dairy-free milk (use coconut milk for AIP)

¼ cup (56 g) ghee, avocado oil or olive oil (for AIP)

1 onion, diced

6 cloves garlic, minced

6½ oz (184 g) artichoke hearts, chopped

2 tbsp (20 g) nutritional yeast

1 tsp sea salt

2 heaping cups (60 g) chopped spinach

1. Pour the cup water into the stainless steel bowl of your Instant Pot and place your sweet potato directly into the water. Secure the lid, close the pressure valve and press the Pressure Cook/Manual button. Use the +/- buttons to adjust until 10 minutes is displayed.

2. Allow the cooking cycle to complete, then quick release the pressure valve and remove the lid once safe to do so. Drain the water. Remove the hot potato, peel it carefully and mash it a bit with a fork. In a deep bowl, blend the dairy-free milk and the sweet potato with an immersion blender. Set it aside.

3. Press the Sauté button and combine the cooking fat, onion, garlic, artichokes, nutritional yeast and sea salt in the Instant Pot bowl. Shift the ingredients for around 5 minutes, until they soften.

4. Add the potato and milk combination and the spinach to the Instant Pot. Stir to combine, then secure the lid, press the Manual/Pressure Cook button and adjust the time with the +/- buttons until it reads 0 minutes. Yes, zero.

5. Allow the dip to cook, then quick release the pressure valve and remove the lid once finished. The dip will continue to thicken as it cools slightly. Serve it warm with veggies.

CREAMY TAHINI ZOODLES

+PALEO +21DSD +LOW CARB +VEGETARIAN

+ MAKES: 2 SERVINGS +
PREP TIME: 5 MINUTES
COOK TIME: 3 MINUTES

One of the challenges of giving up dairy is satisfying the need for creamy-textured foods. These zoodles, made with a simple sauce of garlic and tahini, bring back that rewarding creaminess that is otherwise off limits!

1 cup (240 ml) water

2 zucchini squash, ends trimmed

½ cup (56 g) tahini

¼ cup (60 ml) dairy-free milk

½ tsp sea salt

½ tsp garlic powder

Fresh chives (optional)

1. Begin by pouring the water into the stainless steel bowl of your Instant Pot. Using a spiralizer or julienne slicer, spiral cut your zucchini squash.

2. Place the zoodles in a properly-sized steamer basket and lower them into the Instant Pot. Secure the lid, close the pressure valve and press the Pressure Cook/Manual button. Use the +/- buttons to adjust the time until 3 minutes is displayed.

3. While the zoodles cook, combine all of the remaining ingredients, except the chives, in a bowl and stir well.

4. Once the cooking cycle is complete, quick release the pressure valve and remove the lid once safe to do so. Gently toss the cooked zoodles with the prepared sauce and serve. Garnish with fresh chives, if desired.

SLURP + DRIZZLE

CONDIMENTS ARE KING. My husband and son may argue this point, but luckily I have my daughters to back me up. The saucier the better, I say, and I love a good dipping sauce, salad dressing or topper to my veggies and proteins.

In this chapter, you'll find your basics like Beef, Chicken, Vegetable and Umami Broth (pages 147–152) as well as some delicious sauces like Queso Dip (page 155), Garlic-Infused Ghee (page 163) and Hot Minute Pepper Jelly (page 160). This chapter is dedicated to all the naked proteins and plants that could have used a little extra love and now have it all snuggled into one delicious chapter.

BEEF BROTH

+PALEO +21DSD +LOW CARB +AIP

+ MAKES: 10 SERVINGS +
PREP TIME: 5 MINUTES
COOK TIME: 90 MINUTES

A rich beef broth is delicious on its own in a mug, as well as part of a recipe like gravy or soup. Homemade beef broth has so much more flavor and heartiness, and a single batch of bones can be used multiple times before discarding!

Beef bones

3 tbsp (45 ml) apple cider vinegar

3 large carrots

1 large onion with skin, quartered

3 celery sticks

1 bay leaf

Handful of fresh parsley

2 tsp (10 g) ground pepper

1 tsp ground Himalayan salt

2 tbsp (18 g) garlic, minced

1. Baking the bones at 375°F (190°C) for 30 minutes prior to pressure cooking them helps draw out the marrow, but if you only have access to your pressure cooker, it will still get the job done. To start the broth, place the bones, veggies and seasonings into the Instant Pot. Pour in the apple cider vinegar and then cover with water—the amount you'll need will vary based on the size and quantities of your vegetables.

2. Secure the lid to your Instant Pot, close the pressure valve and press the Pressure Cook/Manual button. Press the +/- buttons to adjust the time to 90 minutes.

3. Once the cooking is complete, quick release the pressure valve and remove the lid once it is safe to do so. Consider freezing the broth in smaller quantities like in ice cube trays and small containers for easier thawing.

CHICKEN BROTH

+PALEO +21DSD +LOW CARB +AIP +KETO

+ MAKES: 10 SERVINGS +
PREP TIME: 5 MINUTES
COOK TIME: 90 MINUTES

Luckily, as time goes on, more store-bought sources of high-quality chicken broth are becoming available. But the truth remains that making it at home is quite simple, and with the Instant Pot, it takes very little time!

Chicken bones

Chicken feet for extra gelatin (optional)

3 large carrots

1 large onion with skin, quartered

3 celery sticks

1 bay leaf

Handful of fresh parsley

2 tsp (10 g) ground pepper

1 tsp ground Himalayan salt

2 tbsp (18 g) garlic, minced

3 tbsp (45 ml) apple cider vinegar

1. To start the broth, place the bones, veggies and seasonings into the Instant Pot. Pour in the apple cider vinegar and then cover with water—the amount you'll need will vary based on the size and quantities of your vegetables.

2. Secure the lid to your Instant Pot, close the pressure valve and press the Pressure Cook/Manual button. Press the +/- buttons to adjust the time to 90 minutes.

3. Once the cooking is complete, quick release the pressure valve and allow the steam to escape. Consider freezing in smaller quantities like ice cube trays and small jars for easier thawing.

NOTE: You can add additional fat to broth like ghee or avocado oil to help increase fat for a ketogenic lifestyle.

VEGETABLE BROTH

+PALEO +21DSD +AIP +LOW CARB +VEGETARIAN

+ **MAKES: 10 SERVINGS** +
PREP TIME: 5 MINUTES
COOK TIME: 30 MINUTES

Store-bought vegetable broths can be a little disappointing, and that's putting it nicely. Making broths at home always adds a touch that mass-produced broths can't quite reach. Toss in the ingredients and a few buttons later, you've got a rich homemade broth in less time than it would take to run to the store and buy!

4 carrots with greens attached

1 large onion with skin, sliced in half

1 tsp onion powder

1 tsp garlic powder

2 bay leaves

2 tbsp (31 g) tomato sauce (omit for AIP)

½ oz (14 g) dried shiitake mushrooms

2 celery stalks

Handful of fresh parsley

2 sprigs fresh dill

1. Add all of the ingredients to the stainless steel bowl of your Instant Pot and fill with water up to the designated limit line.

2. Secure the lid, close the pressure valve and press the Pressure Cook/Manual button. Use the +/- buttons to adjust the time until 30 minutes is displayed.

3. Allow the cooking cycle to complete and then quick release the pressure valve, removing the lid once safe to do so. Strain the veggies and refrigerate the broth for up to a week, freeze it or use it right away.

UMAMI BROTH

+PALEO +21DSD +LOW CARB +AIP +VEGETARIAN

+ MAKES: 6 SERVINGS +
PREP TIME: 5 MINUTES
COOK TIME: 38 MINUTES

Umami, for those unfamiliar with it, is that whole-bodied savory taste that accommodates a delicious lick-your-plate meal. This broth is incredibly versatile and can be used as a base for any gravy or soup!

1 tbsp (14 g) ghee, avocado oil or olive oil

2 tbsp (30 ml) sesame oil

1 large onion, chopped

3 cloves garlic, chopped

6 cups (1.4 L) water

½ oz (14 g) dried shiitake mushrooms

½ oz (14 g) dried oyster mushrooms

1 large carrot

1 tsp apple cider vinegar

½ tsp fish sauce (omit for vegetarian)

3 tbsp (45 ml) coconut aminos

Sea salt to taste

Dill, chives and thyme, for garnish (optional)

1. Drizzle the cooking fat and sesame oil into the stainless steel bowl of your Instant Pot, then add the onion and press the Sauté button. Allow the onion to cook for about 8 minutes, shifting it so it does not burn.

2. Add the remaining ingredients, except for the salt. Press the Keep Warm/Cancel button, secure the lid and close the pressure valve. Press the Pressure Cook/Manual button and then use the +/- buttons to adjust the time until 30 minutes is displayed.

3. Allow the cooking cycle to complete before quick releasing the pressure valve and removing the lid once safe to do so. Strain the broth from the vegetables and add salt to taste. Garnish with herbs, if desired. Use right away or store away refrigerated or frozen for later.

QUESO DIP

+PALEO +21DSD +LOW CARB +VEGETARIAN

MAKES: 10 SERVINGS
PREP TIME: 5 MINUTES
COOK TIME: 7 MINUTES

I sound like a broken record when I reflect upon my Texas roots and obsession with all things cheesy, but since writing *Down South Paleo* and recreating multiple Tex-Mex favorites, I stand by this commitment—if there is a cheese-based recipe to be recreated, I will give it my all.

12 oz (340 g) white-fleshed sweet potato, peeled and chopped

2 cups (480 ml) Vegetable Broth (page 151) or Chicken Broth (page 148)

3 oz (84 g) carrots, chopped

2 tbsp (28 g) ghee

1 tsp garlic powder

1 tsp onion powder

1 tsp sea salt

½ tsp cumin

½ tsp ground chipotle chile

1 tsp chili powder

¼ cup nutritional yeast (optional)

1 (10-oz [285-g]) can diced chilies and tomatoes, drained

Fresh chopped cilantro

1. Add all of the ingredients except for the diced chilies and tomatoes and cilantro to the stainless steel bowl of your Instant Pot. Give them a quick stir and then secure the lid, close the pressure valve and press the Pressure Cook/Manual button. Use the +/- buttons to adjust the time until 7 minutes is displayed.

2. Allow the cooking cycle to complete, then quick release the pressure valve and remove the lid once safe to do so. Use an immersion blender to blend until the dip is smooth and creamy.

3. Add in the drained chilies and tomatoes, stir and top with cilantro to serve.

DATE-SWEETENED BBQ SAUCE

+PALEO

+ MAKES: 10 SERVINGS +
PREP TIME: 2 MINUTES
COOK TIME: 5 MINUTES

Let's be honest, you'll be hard pressed to find a BBQ sauce that doesn't have corn syrup as the first ingredient. Even homemade recipes often call for heaps of sugar. This one is sweetened only with dates, and doesn't even need hours to simmer—just five minutes in your Instant Pot and you're ready to baste with the best of them.

2 tbsp (30 ml) avocado oil or olive oil

1 small onion, diced

5 pitted dates

1 cup (245 g) jarred tomato sauce

1 tsp mustard powder

½ tsp ground black pepper

1 tsp garlic powder

1 tsp onion powder

2 tsp (10 ml) apple cider vinegar

2 tbsp (30 ml) coconut aminos

¼ cup (60 ml) water

1 tsp sea salt

¼ tsp liquid smoke

1. Drizzle the oil into the stainless steel bowl of your Instant Pot and add the onion. Press the Sauté button and cook for 5 minutes, shifting the onion so it doesn't stick or burn.

2. Add the remaining ingredients, give them a quick stir and press the Keep Warm/Cancel button. Secure the lid and close off the pressure valve. Press the Pressure Cook/Manual button and then the +/- buttons until 0 minutes is displayed (yes, zero). It will take a few minutes for the Instant Pot to come to pressure and that will complete the cycle.

3. Allow the cooking cycle to complete, quick release the pressure valve and remove the lid once safe to do so. Use an immersion blender to puree the mixture. If the mixture is too thick, you can thin it out with more coconut aminos.

4. Use as a condiment, baste sauce or marinade. Store in the fridge in a glass jar or use right away.

PESTO "CREAM" SAUCE

+PALEO +21DSD +LOW CARB +VEGETARIAN

It's pretty hard to believe that this gem has no nuts, dairy or thickeners, but believe it! With just a few swaps, you can have your cream sauce and eat it too!

1 small handful (about 2 oz [56 g]) fresh basil leaves

1 (14-oz [385-ml]) can of full-fat coconut milk

¼ cup (56 g) melted ghee

½ tsp sea salt

¼ cup (40 g) pepitas or sunflower seeds, or a combination of both

1 tbsp (9 g) chopped garlic

¼ tsp onion powder

1 to 2 tsp (10 to 20 g) nutritional yeast for cheese flavor (optional)

1. Add all of the ingredients into the stainless steel bowl of your Instant Pot and give them a quick stir. Secure the lid, close the pressure valve and press the Pressure Cook/Manual button. Use the +/- buttons to adjust the time until 2 minutes is displayed.

2. Allow the cooking cycle to complete and then quick release the pressure valve, removing the lid once safe to do so. Use an immersion blender to puree the ingredients. You may need to transfer them to a smaller container so they do not splatter while blending.

3. Serve over mashed cauliflower, zoodles or a protein of your choice.

HOT MINUTE PEPPER JELLY

+PALEO +VEGETARIAN

★ MAKES: 8 SERVINGS ★
PREP TIME: 2 MINUTES
COOK TIME: 5 MINUTES

One of my favorite party foods of all time is pepper jelly with cream cheese on crackers. I've recreated that pepper jelly here, with no added sweeteners other than juice and just the right amount of heat too!

1 cup (240 ml) grape juice

1 cup (240 ml) pomegranate juice

1 red bell pepper, seeded and chopped

Pinch of sea salt

1 jalapeño, seeded and chopped

1 tbsp (15 ml) lemon juice

2 tbsp (28 g) pectin (for vegetarian option) or gelatin (not collagen)

1. Combine all of the ingredients, except the pectin or gelatin, in the stainless steel bowl of your Instant Pot. Close the lid, secure the pressure valve and press the Pressure Cook/Manual button. Use the +/- buttons to adjust the time until 5 minutes is displayed.

2. Allow the cooking cycle to complete and then quick release the pressure valve, removing the lid once safe to do so. Strain the peppers from the juice and transfer the juice to a glass container.

3. Add in your pectin or gelatin and stir until it's dissolved. If using gelatin, you may also use an immersion blender to ensure the gelatin is dissolved. Transfer the container to the refrigerator for a few hours to set. You can keep the jelly chilled for a week or so.

GARLIC-INFUSED GHEE

+PALEO +21DSD +LOW CARB +VEGETARIAN +KETO

★ MAKES: 8 SERVINGS ★
PREP TIME: 0 MINUTES
COOK TIME: 5 MINUTES

Thanks to the military, my family gets to experience a variety of regions. With each move, it's always interesting to learn which ingredients are available and how far I'll have to drive to get them. Ghee is one of those ingredients that is easy to find on the East Coast and nearly impossible to find where I currently live. So guess what? I learned how to make it myself in a snap.

8 oz (225 g) butter (salted or unsalted)

2 tbsp (18 g) minced garlic

1. Place the butter into the stainless steel bowl of your Instant Pot and press the Sauté button, then allow the butter to melt for about 2 minutes.

2. Add in the garlic, then press the Keep Warm/Cancel button, secure the lid and close the pressure valve. Press the Pressure Cook/ Manual button and then the +/- buttons until 3 minutes is displayed

3. Allow the cooking cycle to complete, then quick release the pressure valve and remove the lid once safe to do so. Carefully pour the ghee through a cheesecloth until the milk solids and garlic are removed. You can store it in the fridge or at room temperature.

NOTE: If you are extra sensitive to lactose or casein, this recipe may not be for you.

5 MINUTE EASY ADOBO SAUCE

+PALEO +21DSD +LOW CARB +VEGETARIAN

MAKES: 10 SERVINGS
PREP TIME: 2 MINUTES
COOK TIME: 5 MINUTES

Every time I see a recipe that calls for a small can of chipotle peppers in adobo sauce, I let out a little sigh of frustration. It's a pretty major challenge to hunt down a version of this otherwise easy-to-find grocery staple that isn't made with sketchy ingredients. I finally figured I'd just make it myself, and I'm glad I did—it's pretty darn tasty!

1 cup (245 g) tomato sauce

½ cup (120 ml) apple cider vinegar

½ cup (120 ml) water

4 tbsp (60 g) dried chipotle powder

2 tsp (10 g) cumin

1 tsp garlic powder

½ tsp sea salt

4 dried chipotle peppers

1. Add all of the ingredients in the stainless steel bowl of your Instant Pot and stir to combine. Secure the lid, close the pressure valve and press the Pressure Cook/Manual button. Press the +/- buttons until 5 minutes is displayed.

2. Allow the cooking cycle to complete and then quick release the pressure valve and remove the lid once safe to do so. Store the sauce in the fridge or use it in my Quick Barbacoa with a Kick recipe (page 90).

CREAM-LESS CREAM GRAVY

+PALEO +21DSD +AIP +VEGETARIAN +LOW CARB

+ MAKES: 8 SERVINGS +
PREP TIME: 5 MINUTES ·
COOK TIME: 13 MINUTES

You'd never guess that this thick, creamy brown gravy does not have one sprinkle of flour in it—not even Paleo-approved flour! As they say, the secret's in the sauce!

4 tbsp (56 g) ghee, olive oil or avocado oil

1 onion, sliced thin or diced

10 oz (285 g) white-fleshed sweet potato, peeled and chopped

2 cups (480 ml) Beef Broth (page 147) or Vegetable Broth (page 151)

½ tsp onion powder

½ tsp garlic powder

½ tsp sea salt

1. Spoon your ghee into the stainless steel bowl of your Instant Pot and then press the Sauté button. Add in your onion and sauté, shifting regularly, until it begins to brown, about 8 minutes.

2. Add the remaining ingredients, press the Keep Warm/Cancel button, secure the lid and close the pressure valve. Press the Pressure Cook/Manual button and use the +/- buttons to adjust the time until 5 minutes is displayed.

3. Allow the cooking cycle to complete and then quick release the pressure valve and remove the lid once safe to do so. Use an immersion blender to puree the gravy, first transferring to another bowl if necessary, or use a vertical blender. If your gravy is too thick, you may stir in more broth 1 tablespoon (15 ml) at a time until your desired consistency is reached.

SAUSAGE GRAVY

+PALEO +21DSD +AIP +LOW CARB

Have you ever had a sausage gravy that was so good you didn't even need the biscuit? That's the kind of gravy I like too. This one uses no flours to thicken it, and yet it has the perfect gravy consistency, biscuit or not!

4 tbsp (56 g) ghee or avocado oil (for AIP)

1 lb (450 g) breakfast sausage (be sure to check the spices if AIP)

1 small onion, diced

8 oz (225 g) white-fleshed sweet potato, peeled and sliced

2 cups (480 ml) Beef Broth (page 147)

½ tsp sea salt

½ tsp onion powder

½ tsp garlic powder

1. Press the Sauté feature on your Instant Pot and spoon in the ghee or avocado oil. Add in the breakfast sausage, breaking it up as it cooks, around 8 minutes.

2. Once the sausage is cooked through, remove it from the Instant Pot and set it aside.

3. Add in the remaining ingredients and press the Keep Warm/Cancel button. Secure the lid, close the pressure valve and press the Pressure Cook/Manual button. Use the +/- buttons to adjust the time until 5 minutes is displayed.

4. Allow the cooking cycle to complete and then quick release the pressure valve and remove the lid once safe to do so. Use an immersion blender to puree the hot contents carefully, or transfer them to a vertical blender and puree until creamy.

5. Add the sausage back in and serve as desired.

ACKNOWLEDGMENTS

THANK YOU TO MY FAMILY, who for the second year in a row ate out of an Instant Pot daily for months and never (ok, barely) complained.

THANK YOU TO MY READERS, who supported my other books with such enthusiasm that this book became a must even when I swore high and low that the last book was my finale.

THANK YOU TO PAGE STREET PUBLISHING for convincing me to go for it once more and for cheering me on all the way to the printing press.

THANK YOU TO MY FELLOW AUTHOR FRIENDS in the community who have supported all of my endeavors and have helped promote my work, even in the early days. You know who you are, and I am forever indebted to you.

ABOUT THE AUTHOR

JENNIFER ROBINS is the whole-foodist voice behind the popular food blog Predominantly Paleo, as well as the bestselling author of *Down South Paleo*, *The New Yiddish Kitchen*, *The Paleo Kids Cookbook* and *Paleo Cooking with Your Instant Pot*®. She is also the founder of Legit Bread Company, which is committed to providing high-quality Paleo and nut-free baked goods that are carefully sourced and school safe.

After being diagnosed with several autoimmune conditions and chronic infections, including Lyme disease, Jennifer became gravely ill and mostly homebound. When traditional medical treatments failed to help, Jennifer turned to food for healing. Removing grain, dairy and refined sugars and eating "predominantly Paleo," she started reclaiming her life, one whole-food meal at a time. As a military spouse and mother of three, Jennifer hopes to instill healthy habits in her children in the hope of creating wellness for a lifetime.

+ INDEX +

A

acorn squash, in Migas-Stuffed Acorn Squash, 15
Adobo Sauce
    Quick Barbacoa With A Kick, 90
    recipe for, 164
apple cider vinegar
    Beef Broth, 147
    Chicken Adobo, 32
    Chicken Broth, 148
    Date-Sweetened BBQ Sauce, 156
    5 minute Easy Adobo Sauce, 164
    Mixed Citrus Pulled Pork, 59
    Quick-Pickled Onions, 138
    Shredded Caesar Chicken, 47
    Speedy Sloppy Joes, 86
    Umami Broth, 152
apples, in Liver Lovin' Breakfast Porridge, 16
artichoke hearts, in Hot Minute Spinach + Artichoke Dip, 141
Asian-Inspired Beef + Broccoli, 89
asparagus, in Creamy Asparagus Soup, 137
Autoimmune Protocol (AIP)
    Asian Turkey Lettuce Wraps, 36
    Beef Broth, 147
    Buttered Carrot Bisque, 133
    Chicken Adobo, 32
    Chicken Broth, 148
    Cilantro Lime Shrimp Scampi + Spaghetti Squash, 105
    Cream-Less Cream Gravy, 167
    Creamy Asparagus Soup, 137
    Crust-less Chicken Pot Pie, 35
    Dairy-Free Broccoli "Cheese" Soup, 134
    Egg Roll Meatballs, 51
    Faux Pho, 93
    Golden Milk Breakfast Custard, 24
    Hamburger Soup, 77
    Hearty Clam Chowder, 102
    Hot Minute Spinach + Artichoke Dip, 141
    Irish Lamb Stew, 60
    Lemon Blueberry Pudding Bowl, 20

Liver Lovin' Breakfast Porridge, 16
Minute Mashed Parsnips, 118
Old Country Beet Borsht, 122
Popeye Soup, 126
Quickest French Onion Soup, 130
Quick-Pickled Onions, 138
Sausage + Spinach Soup, 67
Sausage Gravy, 168
Seafood Medley Spread, 106
Southern Sausage + Cabbage, 71
Swedish Meatballs + "Cream" Gravy, 85
Sweet Potato Bacon Hash + Gravy, 19
Thanksgiving Turkey Breast, 48
Vegetable Broth, 151
avocados
    Migas-Stuffed Acorn Squash, 15
    Two-Faced Avocado Eggs, 12

B

bacon
    Cajun Scallops, 97
    Hearty Clam Chowder, 102
    Southern Sausage + Cabbage, 71
    Sweet Potato Bacon Hash + Gravy, 19
bananas, in Liver Lovin' Breakfast Porridge, 16
Barbacoa With a Kick, Quick, 90
basil leaves, in Pesto "Cream" Sauce, 159
bay leaves
    Beef Broth, 147
    Chicken Adobo, 32
    Chicken Broth, 148
    Creamy Crawfish Bisque, 101
    Crust-less Chicken Pot Pie, 35
    Irish Lamb Stew, 60
    Quickest French Onion Soup, 130
    Roux-Less Gumbo, 110
    Sausage + Spinach Soup, 67
    Vegetable Broth, 151
BBQ Sauce, Date-Sweetened, 156
beef, ground

Hamburger Soup, 77
Mexi Meatloaf, 81
No-Bake Shepherd's Pie, 82
Quick + Zesty Enchilada Soup, 78
Southwest Spicy + Sweet Chili, 68
Speedy Sloppy Joes, 86
Swedish Meatballs + "Cream" Gravy, 85
beef bones, in Beef Broth, 147
beef brisket, in Quick Barbacoa With A Kick, 90
Beef Broth
    Asian-Inspired Beef + Broccoli, 89
    Cajun Scallops, 97
    Cream-Less Cream Gravy, 167
    Egg Roll Meatballs, 51
    Faux Pho, 93
    Hamburger Soup, 77
    Irish Lamb Stew, 60
    Mustard Chive Bone-in Pork Chops, 72
    No-Bake Shepherd's Pie, 82
    Old Country Beet Borsht, 122
    Quickest French Onion Soup, 130
    recipe for, 147
    Red Curry Cod, 109
    Roux-Less Gumbo, 110
    Sausage + Spinach Soup, 67
    Sausage Gravy, 168
    Speedy Sloppy Joes, 86
    Swedish Meatballs + "Cream" Gravy, 85
    Thanksgiving Turkey Breast, 48
beef dishes
    Asian-Inspired Beef + Broccoli, 89
    Faux Pho, 93
    Hamburger Soup, 77
    Mexi Meatloaf, 81
    No-Bake Shepherd's Pie, 82
    Quick + Zesty Enchilada Soup, 78
    Quick Barbacoa With A Kick, 90
    Speedy Sloppy Joes, 86
    Swedish Meatballs + "Cream" Gravy, 85

beef steak, in Asian-Inspired Beef + Broccoli, 89
beets
    Liver Lovin' Breakfast Porridge, 16
    Old Country Beet Borsht, 122
bell peppers
    Creamy Crawfish Bisque, 101
    Hot Minute Pepper Jelly, 160
    Quick + Zesty Enchilada Soup, 78
    Roux-Less Gumbo, 110
blueberries, in Lemon Blueberry Pudding Bowl, 20
breakfast fare
    Golden Milk Breakfast Custard, 24
    Lemon Blueberry Pudding Bowl, 20
    Liver Lovin' Breakfast Porridge, 16
    Migas-Stuffed Acorn Squash, 15
    Potato + Egg Breakfast Cups, 27
    Pressure-Cooked Scotch Eggs, 11
    Smoky Spaghetti Squash "Frittata," 23
    Sweet Potato Bacon Hash + Gravy, 19
    Two-Faced Avocado Eggs, 12
broccoli
    Asian-Inspired Beef + Broccoli, 89
    Dairy-Free Broccoli "Cheese" Soup, 134
    Popeye Soup, 126
butter, in Garlic-Infused Ghee, 163
Buttered Carrot Bisque, 133
button mushrooms
    Crab-Stuffed Mushrooms, 98
    Faux Pho, 93
    Loaded Egg Drop Soup, 129
    Tom Kha Gai, 36

C

cabbage, in Southern Sausage + Cabbage, 71
Caesar dressing, 47
Cajun Scallops, 97
Carrot Bisque, Buttered, 133

carrots
    Beef Broth, 147
    Buttered Carrot Bisque, 133
    Chicken Broth, 148
    Chicken Tortilla Soup, 43
    Crust-less Chicken Pot Pie, 35
    Egg Roll Meatballs, 51
    5 minute Taco Meat, 51
    Hamburger Soup, 77
    Irish Lamb Stew, 60
    Loaded Egg Drop Soup, 129
    No-Bake Shepherd's Pie, 82
    Old Country Beet Borsht, 122
    Queso Dip, 155
    Red Curry Cod, 109
    Sausage + Spinach Soup, 67
    Seafood Medley Spread, 106
    Turmeric Tomato Detox Soup, 117
    Umami Broth, 152
    Vegetable Broth, 151
cauliflower
    Crust-less Chicken Pot Pie, 35
    Indian-Inspired "Butter" Cauliflower, 125
    Popeye Soup, 126
    Quick + Zesty Enchilada Soup, 78
    White Chicken Chili, 40
celery
    Beef Broth, 147
    Chicken Broth, 148
    Crust-less Chicken Pot Pie, 35
    Dairy-Free Broccoli "Cheese" Soup, 134
    Hearty Clam Chowder, 102
    Vegetable Broth, 151
Chicken Adobo, 32
chicken and poultry dishes
    Asian Turkey Lettuce Wraps, 36
    Chicken Adobo, 32
    Chicken Marsala, 39
    Chicken Tortilla Soup, 43
    Chicken Yum Yum, 31
    Crust-less Chicken Pot Pie, 35
    5 minute Taco Meat, 51
    Shredded Caesar Chicken, 47
    Tom Kha Gai, 44
    White Chicken Chili, 40
chicken bones, in Chicken Broth, 148
chicken breasts
    Chicken Tortilla Soup, 43
    Crust-less Chicken Pot Pie, 35
    Shredded Caesar Chicken, 47
Chicken Broth
    Cajun Scallops, 97
    Chicken Marsala, 39

Chicken Tortilla Soup, 43
Chicken Yum Yum, 31
Creamy Crawfish Bisque, 101
Crust-less Chicken Pot Pie, 35
Hearty Clam Chowder, 102
Jamaican Jerk Pork Loin, 64
Loaded Egg Drop Soup, 129
Mustard Chive Bone-in Pork Chops, 72
No-Bake Shepherd's Pie, 82
Popeye Soup, 126
Queso Dip, 155
recipe for, 148
Red Curry Cod, 109
Roux-Less Gumbo, 110
Sausage + Spinach Soup, 67
Southern Sausage + Cabbage, 71
Thanksgiving Turkey Breast, 48
Tom Kha Gai, 44
Tomatillo Pork, 63
White Chicken Chili, 40
Chicken Marsala, 39
Chicken Pot Pie, Crust-less, 35
chicken thighs
    Chicken Adobo, 32
    Chicken Yum Yum, 31
    Tom Kha Gai, 44
    White Chicken Chili, 40
Chicken Tortilla Soup, 43
Chicken Yum Yum, 31
Chili
    Southwest Spicy + Sweet, 68
    White Chicken, 40
Chili Lime Salmon, 113
chilies and tomatoes, in Queso Dip, 155
chipotle peppers, in 5 minute Easy Adobo Sauce, 164
chives, in Mustard Chive Bone-in Pork Chops, 72
cilantro
    Cilantro Lime Shrimp Scampi + Spaghetti Squash, 105
    Popeye Soup, 126
    Queso Dip, 155
    Tomatillo Pork, 63
    Turmeric Tomato Detox Soup, 117
    White Chicken Chili, 40
Cilantro Lime Shrimp Scampi + Spaghetti Squash, 105
clams, in Hearty Clam Chowder, 102
coconut aminos
    Asian-Inspired Beef + Broccoli, 89
    Asian Turkey Lettuce Wraps, 36

Chicken Adobo, 32
Chicken Yum Yum, 31
Date-Sweetened BBQ Sauce, 156
Egg Roll Meatballs, 51
Faux Pho, 93
Irish Lamb Stew, 60
Jamaican Jerk Pork Loin, 64
Loaded Egg Drop Soup, 129
No-Bake Shepherd's Pie, 82
Southwest Spicy + Sweet Chili, 68
Speedy Sloppy Joes, 86
Swedish Meatballs + "Cream" Gravy, 85
Umami Broth, 152
coconut cream
    Indian-Inspired "Butter" Cauliflower, 125
    Mustard Chive Bone-in Pork Chops, 72
coconut milk See also milk, dairy-free
    Chicken Adobo, 32
    Creamy Asparagus Soup, 137
    Creamy Crawfish Bisque, 101
    Golden Milk Breakfast Custard, 24
    Hot Minute Spinach + Artichoke Dip, 141
    Lemon Blueberry Pudding Bowl, 20
    Liver Lovin' Breakfast Porridge, 16
    Minute Mashed Parsnips, 118
    Mustard Chive Bone-in Pork Chops, 72
    Pesto "Cream" Sauce, 159
    Popeye Soup, 126
    Red Curry Cod, 109
    Tom Kha Gai, 44
    Turmeric Tomato Detox Soup, 117
cod fillets, in Red Curry Cod, 109
condiments and sauces
    Cream-Less Cream Gravy, 167
    Date-Sweetened BBQ Sauce, 156
    5 minute Easy Adobo Sauce, 164
    Garlic-Infused Ghee, 163
    Hot Minute Pepper Jelly, 160
    Pesto "Cream" Sauce, 159
    Queso Dip, 155
    Sausage Gravy, 168
crabmeat
    Crab-Stuffed Mushrooms, 98
    Seafood Medley Spread, 106
Crab-Stuffed Mushrooms, 98

crawfish, in Creamy Crawfish Bisque, 101
Cream-Less Cream Gravy, 167
Creamy Asparagus Soup, 137
Creamy Crawfish Bisque, 101
Creamy Tahini Zoodles, 142
Crispy Ghee-Licious Smashed Potatoes, 121
Crust-less Chicken Pot Pie, 35

D
Dairy-Free Broccoli "Cheese" Soup, 134
dates
    Chicken Yum Yum, 31
    Chili Lime Salmon, 113
    Date-Sweetened BBQ Sauce, 156
    Golden Milk Breakfast Custard, 24
    Speedy Sloppy Joes, 86
Date-Sweetened BBQ Sauce, 156
Deluxe Sausage Pizza Zucchini Boats, 56
Dijon mustard, in Mustard Chive Bone-in Pork Chops, 72
dill, in Vegetable Broth, 151
dips
    Hot Minute Spinach + Artichoke Dip, 141
    Queso Dip, 155

E
Egg Drop Soup, Loaded, 129
Egg Roll Meatballs, 51
eggs
    Loaded Egg Drop Soup, 129
    Mexi Meatloaf, 81
    Migas-Stuffed Acorn Squash, 15
    Potato + Egg Breakfast Cups, 27
    Pressure-Cooked Scotch Eggs, 11
    Shredded Caesar Chicken, 47
    Smoky Spaghetti Squash "Frittata," 23
    Two-Faced Avocado Eggs, 12
Enchilada Soup, Quick + Zesty, 78

F
Faux Pho, 93
fish and seafood dishes
    Cajun Scallops, 97
    Chili Lime Salmon, 113
    Cilantro Lime Shrimp Scampi + Spaghetti Squash, 105
    Crab-Stuffed Mushrooms, 98

Creamy Crawfish Bisque, 101
Hearty Clam Chowder, 102
Red Curry Cod, 109
Roux-Less Gumbo, 110
Seafood Medley Spread, 106
Umami Broth, 152
fish broth, in Red Curry Cod, 109
fish sauce
    Faux Pho, 93
    Shredded Caesar Chicken, 47
    Tom Kha Gai, 44
5 minute Easy Adobo Sauce, 164
5 minute Taco Meat, 51
French Onion Soup, Quickest,
    130

G
garlic
    Asian-Inspired Beef +
        Broccoli, 89
    Asian Turkey Lettuce Wraps,
        36
    Beef Broth, 147
    Buttered Carrot Bisque, 133
    Chicken Adobo, 32
    Chicken Broth, 148
    Cilantro Lime Shrimp Scampi
        + Spaghetti Squash, 105
    Creamy Asparagus Soup, 137
    Creamy Crawfish Bisque, 101
    Crust-less Chicken Pot Pie, 35
    Dairy-Free Broccoli "Cheese"
        Soup, 134
    5 minute Taco Meat, 51
    Garlic-Infused Ghee, 163
    Hot Minute Spinach +
        Artichoke Dip, 141
    Indian-Inspired "Butter"
        Cauliflower, 125
    Jamaican Jerk Pork Loin, 64
    Loaded Egg Drop Soup, 129
    Mixed Citrus Pulled Pork, 59
    Mustard Chive Bone-in Pork
        Chops, 72
    Pesto "Cream" Sauce, 159
    Popeye Soup, 126
    Quickest French Onion Soup,
        130
    Quick-Pickled Onions, 138
    Sausage + Spinach Soup, 67
    Southwest Spicy + Sweet
        Chili, 68
    Umami Broth, 152
    White Chicken Chili, 40
Garlic-Infused Ghee, 163
gelatin
    Crab-Stuffed Mushrooms, 98
    Egg Roll Meatballs, 51
    Golden Milk Breakfast
        Custard, 24

Hot Minute Pepper Jelly, 160
Lemon Blueberry Pudding
    Bowl, 20
Mexi Meatloaf, 81
Seafood Medley Spread, 106
Swedish Meatballs + "Cream"
    Gravy, 85
Ghee, Garlic-Infused, 163
ginger
    Egg Roll Meatballs, 51
    Tom Kha Gai, 44
Golden Milk Breakfast Custard,
    24
grape juice
    Hot Minute Pepper Jelly, 160
    Lemon Blueberry Pudding
        Bowl, 20
gravy
    Cream-Less Cream Gravy, 167
    Sausage Gravy, 168
    Swedish Meatballs + "Cream"
        Gravy, 85
Gumbo, Roux-Less, 110

H
Hamburger Soup, 77
Hearty Clam Chowder, 102
Hot Minute Pepper Jelly, 160
Hot Minute Spinach + Artichoke
    Dip, 141

I
Indian-Inspired "Butter"
    Cauliflower, 125
Irish Lamb Stew, 60

J
jalapeño peppers
    Hot Minute Pepper Jelly, 160
    Mixed Citrus Pulled Pork, 59
    Southwest Spicy + Sweet
        Chili, 68
    Tomatillo Pork, 63
Jamaican Jerk Pork Loin, 64

K
Keto diet
    Asian Turkey Lettuce Wraps,
        36
    Chicken Adobo, 32
    Chicken Broth, 148
    Chicken Tortilla Soup, 43
    Crab-Stuffed Mushrooms, 98
    Creamy Asparagus Soup, 137
    Egg Roll Meatballs, 51
    Faux Pho, 93
    Garlic-Infused Ghee, 163
    Mustard Chive Bone-in Pork
        Chops, 72

Pressure-Cooked Scotch
    Eggs, 11
Quickest French Onion Soup,
    130
Sausage + Spinach Soup, 67
Shredded Caesar Chicken, 47
Southern Sausage +
    Cabbage, 71
Thanksgiving Turkey Breast,
    48
Tom Kha Gai, 44
Tomatillo Pork, 63
Two-Faced Avocado Eggs, 12
kielbasa
    Roux-Less Gumbo, 110
    Southern Sausage +
        Cabbage, 71

L
lamb, in Irish Lamb Stew, 60
Lemon Blueberry Pudding Bowl,
    20
lemongrass, in Tom Kha Gai, 44
lemons and lemon juice
    Creamy Asparagus Soup, 137
    Hot Minute Pepper Jelly, 160
    Lemon Blueberry Pudding
        Bowl, 20
    Mixed Citrus Pulled Pork, 59
    Shredded Caesar Chicken, 47
lettuce
    Asian Turkey Lettuce Wraps,
        36
    Shredded Caesar Chicken, 47
limes and lime juice
    Chili Lime Salmon, 113
    Cilantro Lime Shrimp Scampi
        + Spaghetti Squash, 105
    Jamaican Jerk Pork Loin, 64
    Quick Barbacoa With A Kick,
        90
    Tom Kha Gai, 44
    Tomatillo Pork, 63
Liver Lovin' Breakfast Porridge,
    16
Loaded Egg Drop Soup, 129
Low Carb diet
    Asian-Inspired Beef +
        Broccoli, 89
    Asian Turkey Lettuce Wraps,
        36
    Beef Broth, 147
    Cajun Scallops, 97
    Chicken Adobo, 32
    Chicken Broth, 148
    Chicken Tortilla Soup, 43
    Chili Lime Salmon, 113
    Cilantro Lime Shrimp Scampi
        + Spaghetti Squash, 105

Crab-Stuffed Mushrooms, 98
Cream-Less Cream Gravy, 167
Creamy Asparagus Soup, 137
Creamy Crawfish Bisque, 101
Creamy Tahini Zoodles, 142
Crust-less Chicken Pot Pie, 35
Dairy-Free Broccoli "Cheese"
    Soup, 134
Deluxe Sausage Pizza
    Zucchini Boats, 56
Egg Roll Meatballs, 51
Faux Pho, 93
5 minute Easy Adobo Sauce,
    164
5 minute Taco Meat, 51
Garlic-Infused Ghee, 163
Hamburger Soup, 77
Hearty Clam Chowder, 102
Hot Minute Spinach +
    Artichoke Dip, 141
Indian-Inspired "Butter"
    Cauliflower, 125
Jamaican Jerk Pork Loin, 64
Loaded Egg Drop Soup, 129
Mexi Meatloaf, 81
Migas-Stuffed Acorn Squash,
    15
Minute Mashed Parsnips, 118
Mustard Chive Bone-in Pork
    Chops, 72
Old Country Beet Borsht, 122
Pesto "Cream" Sauce, 159
Popeye Soup, 126
Pressure-Cooked Scotch
    Eggs, 11
Queso Dip, 155
Quick + Zesty Enchilada
    Soup, 78
Quick Barbacoa With A Kick,
    90
Quickest French Onion Soup,
    130
Quick-Pickled Onions, 138
Red Curry Cod, 109
Roux-Less Gumbo, 110
Sausage + Spinach Soup, 67
Sausage Gravy, 168
Seafood Medley Spread, 106
Shredded Caesar Chicken, 47
Smoky Spaghetti Squash
    "Frittata," 23
Southern Sausage +
    Cabbage, 71
Southwest Spicy + Sweet
    Chili, 68
Swedish Meatballs + "Cream"
    Gravy, 85
Thanksgiving Turkey Breast,
    48
Tom Kha Gai, 44

Tomatillo Pork, 63
Turmeric Tomato Detox Soup, 117
Two-Faced Avocado Eggs, 12
Vegetable Broth, 151
White Chicken Chili, 40

M
marinara sauce, in Deluxe Sausage Pizza Zucchini Boats, 56
Marsala wine, in Chicken Marsala, 39
mashed potatoes, 82
mayonnaise, in Crab-Stuffed Mushrooms, 98
meatballs
    Egg Roll Meatballs, 51
    Swedish Meatballs + "Cream" Gravy, 85
Mexi Meatloaf, 81
Migas-Stuffed Acorn Squash, 15
milk, dairy-free *See also* coconut milk
    Creamy Tahini Zoodles, 142
    Hot Minute Spinach + Artichoke Dip, 141
Minute Mashed Parsnips, 118
Mixed Citrus Pulled Pork, 59
mushrooms
    Asian Turkey Lettuce Wraps, 36
    button, 36
    Chicken Marsala, 39
    Crab-Stuffed Mushrooms, 98
    Faux Pho, 93
    Loaded Egg Drop Soup, 129
    oyster, 44
    Tom Kha Gai, 44
    Umami Broth, 152
    Vegetable Broth, 151
Mustard Chive Bone-in Pork Chops, 72

N
No-Bake Shepherd's Pie, 82
nutritional yeast
    Dairy-Free Broccoli "Cheese" Soup, 134
    Hot Minute Spinach + Artichoke Dip, 141
    Pesto "Cream" Sauce, 159

O
okra, in Roux-Less Gumbo, 110
Old Country Beet Borsht, 122
onions
    Asian-Inspired Beef + Broccoli, 89

Asian Turkey Lettuce Wraps, 36
Beef Broth, 147
Buttered Carrot Bisque, 133
Cajun Scallops, 97
Chicken Broth, 148
Chicken Marsala, 39
Chicken Tortilla Soup, 43
Cream-Less Cream Gravy, 167
Creamy Asparagus Soup, 137
Creamy Crawfish Bisque, 101
Crust-less Chicken Pot Pie, 35
Dairy-Free Broccoli "Cheese" Soup, 134
Date-Sweetened BBQ Sauce, 156
Deluxe Sausage Pizza Zucchini Boats, 56
Egg Roll Meatballs, 51
Faux Pho, 93
5 minute Taco Meat, 51
Hamburger Soup, 77
Hearty Clam Chowder, 102
Hot Minute Spinach + Artichoke Dip, 141
Indian-Inspired "Butter" Cauliflower, 125
Irish Lamb Stew, 60
Jamaican Jerk Pork Loin, 64
Mexi Meatloaf, 81
Mixed Citrus Pulled Pork, 59
No-Bake Shepherd's Pie, 82
Old Country Beet Borsht, 122
Popeye Soup, 126
Quick + Zesty Enchilada Soup, 78
Quickest French Onion Soup, 130
Quick-Pickled Onions, 138
Red Curry Cod, 109
Roux-Less Gumbo, 110
Sausage + Spinach Soup, 67
Sausage Gravy, 168
Smoky Spaghetti Squash "Frittata," 23
Southern Sausage + Cabbage, 71
Southwest Spicy + Sweet Chili, 68
Speedy Sloppy Joes, 86
Swedish Meatballs + "Cream" Gravy, 85
Sweet Potato Bacon Hash + Gravy, 19
Tomatillo Pork, 63
Turmeric Tomato Detox Soup, 117
Umami Broth, 152
Vegetable Broth, 151

White Chicken Chili, 40
orange juice, in Mixed Citrus Pulled Pork, 59
oyster mushrooms
    Tom Kha Gai, 44
    Umami Broth, 152

P
Paleo diet
    Asian-Inspired Beef + Broccoli, 89
    Asian Turkey Lettuce Wraps, 36
    Beef Broth, 147
    Buttered Carrot Bisque, 133
    Cajun Scallops, 97
    Chicken Adobo, 32
    Chicken Broth, 148
    Chicken Marsala, 39
    Chicken Tortilla Soup, 43
    Chicken Yum Yum, 31
    Chili Lime Salmon, 113
    Cilantro Lime Shrimp Scampi + Spaghetti Squash, 105
    Crab-Stuffed Mushrooms, 98
    Cream-Less Cream Gravy, 167
    Creamy Asparagus Soup, 137
    Creamy Crawfish Bisque, 101
    Creamy Tahini Zoodles, 142
    Crispy Ghee-Licious Smashed Potatoes, 121
    Crust-less Chicken Pot Pie, 35
    Dairy-Free Broccoli "Cheese" Soup, 134
    Date-Sweetened BBQ Sauce, 156
    Deluxe Sausage Pizza Zucchini Boats, 56
    Egg Roll Meatballs, 51
    Faux Pho, 93
    5 minute Easy Adobo Sauce, 164
    5 minute Taco Meat, 51
    Garlic-Infused Ghee, 163
    Golden Milk Breakfast Custard, 24
    Hamburger Soup, 77
    Hearty Clam Chowder, 102
    Hot Minute Pepper Jelly, 160
    Hot Minute Spinach + Artichoke Dip, 141
    Indian-Inspired "Butter" Cauliflower, 125
    Irish Lamb Stew, 60
    Jamaican Jerk Pork Loin, 64
    Lemon Blueberry Pudding Bowl, 20
    Liver Lovin' Breakfast Porridge, 16

Loaded Egg Drop Soup, 129
Mexi Meatloaf, 81
Migas-Stuffed Acorn Squash, 15
Minute Mashed Parsnips, 118
Mixed Citrus Pulled Pork, 59
Mustard Chive Bone-in Pork Chops, 72
No-Bake Shepherd's Pie, 82
Old Country Beet Borsht, 122
Pesto "Cream" Sauce, 159
Popeye Soup, 126
Potato + Egg Breakfast Cups, 27
Pressure-Cooked Scotch Eggs, 11
Queso Dip, 155
Quick + Zesty Enchilada Soup, 78
Quick Barbacoa With A Kick, 90
Quickest French Onion Soup, 130
Quick-Pickled Onions, 138
Red Curry Cod, 109
Roux-Less Gumbo, 110
Sausage + Spinach Soup, 67
Sausage Gravy, 168
Seafood Medley Spread, 106
Shredded Caesar Chicken, 47
Smoky Spaghetti Squash "Frittata," 23
Southern Sausage + Cabbage, 71
Southwest Spicy + Sweet Chili, 68
Speedy Sloppy Joes, 86
Swedish Meatballs + "Cream" Gravy, 85
Sweet Potato Bacon Hash + Gravy, 19
Thanksgiving Turkey Breast, 48
Tom Kha Gai, 44
Tomatillo Pork, 63
Turmeric Tomato Detox Soup, 117
Two-Faced Avocado Eggs, 12
Vegetable Broth, 151
White Chicken Chili, 40
Paleo tortillas, in Quick Barbacoa With A Kick, 90
parsley
    Beef Broth, 147
    Chicken Broth, 148
    Vegetable Broth, 151
parsnips, in Minute Mashed Parsnips, 118

pectin, in Hot Minute Pepper Jelly, 160
pepitas, in Pesto "Cream" Sauce, 159
Pepper Jelly, Hot Minute, 160
pepperoni, in Deluxe Sausage Pizza Zucchini Boats, 56
peppers
    Creamy Crawfish Bisque, 101
    5 minute Easy Adobo Sauce, 164
    Hot Minute Pepper Jelly, 160
    Mixed Citrus Pulled Pork, 59
    Quick + Zesty Enchilada Soup, 78
    Roux-Less Gumbo, 110
    Southwest Spicy + Sweet Chili, 68
    Tomatillo Pork, 63
Pesto "Cream" Sauce, 159
Pho, Faux, 93
pineapple, in Mixed Citrus Pulled Pork, 59
pomegranate juice
    Hot Minute Pepper Jelly, 160
    Liver Lovin' Breakfast Porridge, 16
Popeye Soup, 126
pork, ground, in Egg Roll Meatballs, 51
pork and lamb dishes
    Deluxe Sausage Pizza Zucchini Boats, 56
    Egg Roll Meatballs, 55
    Irish Lamb Stew, 60
    Jamaican Jerk Pork Loin, 64
    Mixed Citrus Pulled Pork, 59
    Mustard Chive Bone-in Pork Chops, 72
    Sausage + Spinach Soup, 67
    Southern Sausage + Cabbage, 71
    Southwest Spicy + Sweet Chili, 68
    Tomatillo Pork, 63
pork broth
    Mustard Chive Bone-in Pork Chops, 72
    Tomatillo Pork, 63
pork chops, in Mustard Chive Bone-in Pork Chops, 72
pork loin
    Jamaican Jerk Pork Loin, 64
    Tomatillo Pork, 63
pork roast, in Mixed Citrus Pulled Pork, 59
Potato + Egg Breakfast Cups, 27
potatoes

Crispy Ghee-Licious Smashed Potatoes, 121
Hamburger Soup, 77
Hearty Clam Chowder, 102
Irish Lamb Stew, 60
No-Bake Shepherd's Pie, 82
Potato + Egg Breakfast Cups, 27
Pressure-Cooked Scotch Eggs, 11
Pulled Pork, Mixed Citrus, 59

Q
Queso Dip, 155
Quick + Zesty Enchilada Soup, 78
Quick Barbacoa With A Kick, 90
Quickest French Onion Soup, 130
Quick-Pickled Onions, 138

R
raspberries, in Liver Lovin' Breakfast Porridge, 16
Red Curry Cod, 109
red onions, in Deluxe Sausage Pizza Zucchini Boats, 56
romaine lettuce
    Asian Turkey Lettuce Wraps, 36
    Shredded Caesar Chicken, 47
Roux-Less Gumbo, 110

S
salmon
    Chili Lime Salmon, 113
    Seafood Medley Spread, 106
salsa
    Chicken Tortilla Soup, 43
    Mexi Meatloaf, 81
sausage
    Deluxe Sausage Pizza Zucchini Boats, 56
    Pressure-Cooked Scotch Eggs, 11
    Roux-Less Gumbo, 110
    Sausage + Spinach Soup, 67
    Sausage Gravy, 168
    Southern Sausage + Cabbage, 71
    Southwest Spicy + Sweet Chili, 68
Sausage + Spinach Soup, 67
Sausage Gravy, 168
scallops, in Cajun Scallops, 97
Scotch Eggs, Pressure Cooked, 11
seafood *See* fish and seafood dishes
seafood broth, in Roux-Less Gumbo, 110

Seafood Medley Spread, 106
Shepherd's Pie, No-Bake, 82
sherry cooking wine, in Creamy Crawfish Bisque, 101
shiitake mushrooms
    Umami Broth, 152
    Vegetable Broth, 151
Shredded Caesar Chicken, 47
shrimp
    Cilantro Lime Shrimp Scampi + Spaghetti Squash, 105
    Roux-Less Gumbo, 110
Smoky Spaghetti Squash "Frittata," 23
soups and stews
    Beef Broth, 147
    Buttered Carrot Bisque, 133
    Chicken Broth, 148
    Chicken Tortilla Soup, 43
    Creamy Asparagus Soup, 137
    Creamy Crawfish Bisque, 101
    Dairy-Free Broccoli "Cheese" Soup, 134
    Faux Pho, 93
    Hamburger Soup, 77
    Hearty Clam Chowder, 102
    Irish Lamb Stew, 60
    Loaded Egg Drop Soup, 129
    Old Country Beet Borsht, 122
    Popeye Soup, 126
    Quick + Zesty Enchilada Soup, 78
    Quickest French Onion Soup, 130
    Sausage + Spinach Soup, 67
    Southwest Spicy + Sweet Chili, 68
    Tom Kha Gai, 44
    Turmeric Tomato Detox Soup, 117
    Umami Broth, 152
    Vegetable Broth, 151
Southern Sausage + Cabbage, 71
Southwest Spicy + Sweet Chili, 68
spaghetti squash
    Cilantro Lime Shrimp Scampi + Spaghetti Squash, 105
    Smoky Spaghetti Squash "Frittata," 23
Speedy Sloppy Joes, 86
spinach
    Hot Minute Spinach + Artichoke Dip, 141
    Popeye Soup, 126
    Sausage + Spinach Soup, 67
squash
    Cilantro Lime Shrimp Scampi + Spaghetti Squash, 105

Creamy Tahini Zoodles, 142
Deluxe Sausage Pizza Zucchini Boats, 56
Migas-Stuffed Acorn Squash, 15
Smoky Spaghetti Squash "Frittata," 23
sunflower seeds, in Pesto "Cream" Sauce, 159
Swedish Meatballs + "Cream" Gravy, 85
Sweet Potato Bacon Hash + Gravy, 19
sweet potatoes
    Cream-Less Cream Gravy, 167
    Crust-less Chicken Pot Pie, 35
    Dairy-Free Broccoli "Cheese" Soup, 134
    Hamburger Soup, 77
    Hearty Clam Chowder, 102
    Hot Minute Spinach + Artichoke Dip, 141
    Irish Lamb Stew, 60
    Mexi Meatloaf, 81
    Queso Dip, 155
    Sausage Gravy, 168
    Seafood Medley Spread, 106
    Southwest Spicy + Sweet Chili, 68
    Swedish Meatballs + "Cream" Gravy, 85
    Sweet Potato Bacon Hash + Gravy, 19

T
tahini, in Creamy Tahini Zoodles, 142
Thanksgiving Turkey Breast, 48
thyme, in Quickest French Onion Soup, 130
Tom Kha Gai, 44
Tomatillo Pork, 63
tomatillos, in Tomatillo Pork, 63
tomato sauce
    Chicken Yum Yum, 31
    Date-Sweetened BBQ Sauce, 156
    5 minute Easy Adobo Sauce, 164
    5 minute Taco Meat, 51
    Indian-Inspired "Butter" Cauliflower, 125
    Quick + Zesty Enchilada Soup, 78
    Red Curry Cod, 109
    Roux-Less Gumbo, 110
    Speedy Sloppy Joes, 86
    Vegetable Broth, 151
tomatoes, crushed

Southwest Spicy + Sweet Chili, 68

Turmeric Tomato Detox Soup, 117

tomatoes and chilies, in Queso Dip, 155

tortillas, in Quick Barbacoa With A Kick, 90

tuna, in Seafood Medley Spread, 106

turkey
Asian Turkey Lettuce Wraps, 36

5 minute Taco Meat, 51

Thanksgiving Turkey Breast, 48

Turkey Broth, in Thanksgiving Turkey Breast, 48

turmeric
Golden Milk Breakfast Custard, 24

Turmeric Tomato Detox Soup, 117

Turmeric Tomato Detox Soup, 117

21 Day Sugar Detox (21DSD)
Asian-Inspired Beef + Broccoli, 89

Asian Turkey Lettuce Wraps, 36

Beef Broth, 147

Buttered Carrot Bisque, 133

Cajun Scallops, 97

Chicken Adobo, 32

Chicken Broth, 148

Chicken Tortilla Soup, 43

Chili Lime Salmon, 113

Cilantro Lime Shrimp Scampi + Spaghetti Squash, 105

Crab-Stuffed Mushrooms, 98

Cream-Less Cream Gravy, 167

Creamy Asparagus Soup, 137

Creamy Crawfish Bisque, 101

Creamy Tahini Zoodles, 142

Crispy Ghee-Licious Smashed Potatoes, 121

Crust-less Chicken Pot Pie, 35

Dairy-Free Broccoli "Cheese" Soup, 134

Deluxe Sausage Pizza Zucchini Boats, 56

Egg Roll Meatballs, 51

Faux Pho, 93

5 minute Easy Adobo Sauce, 164

5 minute Taco Meat, 51

Garlic-Infused Ghee, 163

Hamburger Soup, 77

Hearty Clam Chowder, 102

Hot Minute Spinach + Artichoke Dip, 141

Indian-Inspired "Butter" Cauliflower, 125

Irish Lamb Stew, 60

Jamaican Jerk Pork Loin, 64

Loaded Egg Drop Soup, 129

Mexi Meatloaf, 81

Migas-Stuffed Acorn Squash, 15

Minute Mashed Parsnips, 118

Mustard Chive Bone-in Pork Chops, 72

No-Bake Shepherd's Pie, 82

Old Country Beet Borsht, 122

Pesto "Cream" Sauce, 159

Popeye Soup, 126

Potato + Egg Breakfast Cups, 27

Pressure-Cooked Scotch Eggs, 11

Queso Dip, 155

Quick + Zesty Enchilada Soup, 78

Quick Barbacoa With A Kick, 90

Quickest French Onion Soup, 130

Quick-Pickled Onions, 138

Red Curry Cod, 109

Roux-Less Gumbo, 110

Sausage + Spinach Soup, 67

Sausage Gravy, 168

Seafood Medley Spread, 106

Shredded Caesar Chicken, 47

Smoky Spaghetti Squash "Frittata," 23

Southern Sausage + Cabbage, 71

Southwest Spicy + Sweet Chili, 68

Swedish Meatballs + "Cream" Gravy, 85

Sweet Potato Bacon Hash + Gravy, 19

Thanksgiving Turkey Breast, 48

Tom Kha Gai, 44

Tomatillo Pork, 63

Turmeric Tomato Detox Soup, 117

Two-Faced Avocado Eggs, 12

Vegetable Broth, 151

White Chicken Chili, 40

Two-Faced Avocado Eggs, 12

U
Umami Broth
Cajun Scallops, 97

Quickest French Onion Soup, 130

recipe for, 152

V
Vegetable Broth
Buttered Carrot Bisque, 133

Cream-Less Cream Gravy, 167

Creamy Asparagus Soup, 137

Dairy-Free Broccoli "Cheese" Soup, 134

Loaded Egg Drop Soup, 129

Old Country Beet Borsht, 122

Queso Dip, 155

Quickest French Onion Soup, 130

recipe for, 151

Roux-Less Gumbo, 110

Turmeric Tomato Detox Soup, 117

Vegetable Broth, 151

vegetable dishes
Buttered Carrot Bisque, 133

Creamy Asparagus Soup, 137

Creamy Tahini Zoodles, 142

Crispy Ghee-Licious Smashed Potatoes, 121

Dairy-Free Broccoli "Cheese" Soup, 134

Hot Minute Spinach + Artichoke Dip, 141

Indian-Inspired "Butter" Cauliflower, 125

Loaded Egg Drop Soup, 129

Minute Mashed Parsnips, 118

Old Country Beet Borsht, 122

Popeye Soup, 126

Quickest French Onion Soup, 130

Quick-Pickled Onions, 138

Turmeric Tomato Detox Soup, 117

Vegetarian diet
Buttered Carrot Bisque, 133

Cream-Less Cream Gravy, 167

Creamy Asparagus Soup, 137

Creamy Tahini Zoodles, 142

Dairy-Free Broccoli "Cheese" Soup, 134

5 minute Easy Adobo Sauce, 164

Garlic-Infused Ghee, 163

Hot Minute Pepper Jelly, 160

Hot Minute Spinach + Artichoke Dip, 141

Indian-Inspired "Butter" Cauliflower, 125

Liver Lovin' Breakfast Porridge, 16

Loaded Egg Drop Soup, 129

Migas-Stuffed Acorn Squash, 15

Old Country Beet Borsht, 122

Pesto "Cream" Sauce, 159

Potato + Egg Breakfast Cups, 27

Queso Dip, 155

Quickest French Onion Soup, 130

Quick-Pickled Onions, 138

Smoky Spaghetti Squash "Frittata," 23

Turmeric Tomato Detox Soup, 117

Two-Faced Avocado Eggs, 12

vinegar See apple cider vinegar

W
White Chicken Chili, 40

wine
Chicken Marsala, 39

Creamy Crawfish Bisque, 101

Z
zucchini
Creamy Tahini Zoodles, 142

Deluxe Sausage Pizza Zucchini Boats, 56